BRITAIN
IN OLD PHOTOGRAPHS

LLANDUDNO

PAST & PRESENT

JIM ROBERTS

SUTTON PUBLISHING

Sutton Publishing Limited
Phoenix Mill · Thrupp · Stroud
Gloucestershire · GL5 2BU

First published 2002

Reprinted in 2002

Copyright © Jim Roberts, 2002

Title page photograph: Goats at sunset on the
Great Orme.

British Library Cataloguing in Publication Data
A catalogue record for this book is available from the
British Library.

ISBN 0-7509-2903-0

Typeset in 10.5/13.5 Photina.
Typesetting and origination by
Sutton Publishing Limited.
Printed and bound in England by
J.H. Haynes & Co. Ltd, Sparkford.

> *To my wife and family,*
> *and to the memory of David Hughes,*
> *Antiquarian Bookseller, and everyone's friend.*

Llandudno from the Great Orme, *Illustrated Times* 1862.

CONTENTS

On 14 July 1959 Llandudno Urban District Council was granted its Armorial Bearings by Letters Patent. The motto *Hardd, Hafan, Hedd* is a Welsh translation of the expression used by Queen Elizabeth of Roumania who visited the town in 1890. Pursued everywhere by gawping crowds, she described Llandudno as a 'Beautiful haven of peace'.

The shield shows the church of St Tudno overlooking the sea, with two of the lions from the arms of the Welsh Princes of Gwynedd. The dragon crest holds the shield of the Mostyn family and the hill on which the dragon stands bears two spur-rowels from the arms of the Bishop of Bangor, who had a palace on the hill at Gogarth (Great Orme).

A BRIEF HISTORY OF LLANDUDNO

Bishop's Quarry, 2001.

Evidence of Llandudno's prehistoric past has accumulated over the years. The Ormes themselves consist of carboniferous limestone laid down some three hundred million years ago. There is fossil evidence, from the Bishop's Quarry, of the rise and fall of the sea levels and the folding and buckling of the earth's surface raising what was once the seabed to the Orme's summit. The ice ages, which occurred between 60,000 and 10,000 BP, left glacial erratics on the slopes of the Great Orme. The enormous glaciers that formed the Snowdon Range and the Vale of Conway swept majestically to the sea at this point to join the Irish Sea ice, along with breakaway icebergs from the Scottish icefields. These cataclysmic geological events have, of course, been the foundations and the determinants of the town's history. The height and lack of trees on the Ormes were what probably attracted the earliest human inhabitants to the area. Elevation was a singular defensive advantage in what was presumably a society of territorially warring tribes, and the lack of trees presented uninterrupted look-out points and space for hut building. Recent evidence and the finds of Kendrick (see later) suggest that the area has probably been inhabited since about 12,000 BP (before the present). Tools, pottery (Beaker) and various artefacts of the Bronze Age (4,300 BP and 3,700 BP) have been found in the nooks and crannies of the Orme which is now regarded as an archaeological site of world importance. Further consideration is given to this when we consider copper mining later on in the book.

Cottage Loaf glacial erratic.

Cromlech on the Orme's Head.

The view from Pen-y-Dinas today.

One cromlech remains on the Orme and is further evidence of early habitation, but there were other megalithic tombs that were removed as the town developed. The construction of Marine Drive was responsible for the loss of several of them.

The Romans appear to have been attracted to areas rich in metallic mineral ores. In Wales they homed in on copper and gold in Snowdonia, lead and zinc in Flintshire, and in Llandudno its copper ore probably attracted them, though some lead was excavated. From their bases at Chester, Segontium and Caerhun in the Conway Valley they came, it is believed, to exploit Llandudno's mineral wealth though hard evidence that they did is difficult to find. There was no Welsh subjugation in the truest sense because the nation was too adept at the fine art of guerrilla warfare. Certainly coin hoards, Romano-British pottery fragments, various tools of the second century AD and a massive 5,000 or so hoard of coins found in roadworks close to the Little Orme are all conclusive evidence of Roman presence in the area.

The Iron Age hut circles on Pen-y-Dinas are arranged unusually in straight lines and it has been suggested that this is Roman influence, the huts being the homes of miners employed by the Romans. It has also been suggested that the small denomination coin hoard from the Little Orme find was miners' wages. Others would argue that this is, perhaps, adding two and two together to make more than four.

Viking raids on mainland Britain started in about 760 and increased in size and intensity from AD 800 to 900. North Wales and the Wirral were particularly prone to receiving these unwelcome visitors for reasons that will be explained later. They were a constant threat to the city of Chester, and Archaeologists there have uncovered Viking skull pits containing gruesome remains.

When one considers the invasions and incursions of the Vikings into North Wales it is too easy to conclude that they had travelled long journeys from various archipelagos in Northern Europe. Actually, they had had a relatively short journey from either Ireland (they had bases in Dublin, Waterford and Limerick) or the Isle of Man which was a dependency of Denmark from 860 to 1266. The duration of their journey leads one to conclude that the Vikings were the tenth-century equivalent of the daytripper.

Rising out of the sea-mist, the two headlands of Llandudno Bay reminded them of serpents. Orme's Head is a Viking name (*orma* a serpent) and may be compared with Worm's Head in South Wales. Nowadays, the promenader looking out to sea is more likely to think that the Great Orme on his left is a crocodile basking on a rock, and the Little Orme to his right is an elephant half immersed in the sea.

For centuries the village at the foot of the Orme led a quiet and peaceful, if not prosperous, existence. The inhabitants made a meagre living from fishing, grazing, and sporadic mining. Christianity had come with St Tudno's little monastic community sometime in the sixth century, and the marauding Vikings were still adding a little unwanted excitement.

St Tudno's church, an engraving from the early nineteenth century.

Ruins of the Bishop's Palace, *c.* 1880.

Mostyn family crest (My help is in the Lord).

In the thirteenth century a grand palace of medieval bishops was built on the West Shore, an area given to the Bishopric of Bangor by Edward I following the christening of Edward II at Caernarfon after the 1282 conquest. In the ruins, signs of a conflagration show that perhaps it fell victim to Owain Glyndwr in the 1405 rebellion. In 1536, the traveller and historian Leland describes the palace as being 'almost clene down', so the destruction is not recent and not owing to the encroaching sea (which was probably a few fields off at the time). There is a path from St Tudno's church to the Bishop's Palace, green all the year round (because trodden by righteous men dripping with holy water, but more likely manured by sheep and goats and watered by underground springs).

In the Dark Ages following the departure of the Romans there appears to have been little demand for copper, so it is likely that the mining industry on the Orme declined almost to the point of non-existence. It was not until the late eighteenth and early nineteenth centuries that mining resumed an increased level of importance under the demands of two landlords: the Bishop of Bangor, and the Mostyn family. The Mostyns were the most prominent mining family in North Wales; coal and lead in Flintshire, and copper from Llandudno swelled their bulging coffers. Underlining the whole history of the town is a confidence trick perpetrated by the church and nobility. The Rt Revd Christopher Bethel, Lord Bishop of Bangor and Lord of the Manor of Gogarth, and Edward Mostyn, MP for Flintshire, son of Baron Mostyn and nephew of Lady Champneys, schemed to acquire the almost 1,000 acres of parish common land on which Llandudno now stands. They succeeded when Edward Mostyn introduced the Eglwysrhos, Llandudno and Llangystenin Enclosure Bill to Parliament, which became law in 1843. The owners of the common land did nothing but meekly accept the 30 square yards they were given on which to sink a communal well. In the 150 years or so since this time Mostyn Estates occasionally surprises the town with its munificence, and returns to the community a small piece of what is theirs anyway.

The elevation of the Mostyn family, which has made them so important, was owed to two successful marriages which brought them the estates of Gloddaeth in the 1450s and Bodysgallen in the eighteenth century, which they added to the land they owned in and around Flintshire. Because of their ownership of the ground leases of most of its property, the estate controls a great deal of the town, and is still trying to exercise its influence on the town's future development, though of late this influence is being questioned and, on occasions, resisted.

When considering the names of the great and the good who have contributed to the history of the town, accounts usually begin with the collaboration between John Williams and Lord Mostyn, and a famous meeting in a fisherman's hut where the town was planned. However, before this, news was spreading about the area through the pages of the *Liverpool Mercury*. A native of the village of

Victorian visitors on the Great Orme, *c.* 1880.

Llandudno was Revd John Pritchard, who became a minister at Llangollen. He subsequently married a sister-in-law of the Editor of the *Mercury*, John Smith. Williams persuaded Smith to visit Llandudno, and he travelled to the town from Liverpool by steamship as there was no other way to get there easily in those days. It would be putting it mildly to suggest that the newspaperman was taken with the area. 'You have not told us one half of the beauties and attractions of Llandudno as a watering place; it is the most desirable spot on the shores of Britain, and easy to reach from England by sea or land.' Several articles written by Smith enthusing about Llandudno in the pages of the *Mercury* followed this, helping to disseminate the attractions of the area to a much wider public. To this day the town has a particular attraction for the people of Merseyside, who visit in large numbers annually. It would be true to say, also, that the articles influenced the Mostyn family, who were probably anxious to capitalise on the piece of marsh and scrubland they had seized and enclosed.

These small beginnings led to hordes of people arriving at the relatively primitive village, and the problems associated with their arrival had to be solved. The photograph on the previous page shows early Victorian visitors on the slopes of the Orme in about 1880. Before the railway came to North Wales in 1848 it was not easy to get to the area overland. Most visitors arrived by boat. There was, as yet, no pier, so people were rowed to the shore and carried to dry land by the strong arms of the local porters. They had to be fed and watered and, if they wished to prolong their visit, accommodation had to be supplied. This became Llandudno's raison d'etre. A new industry was added to mining and fishing; tourism was to become the town's overriding concern, and the town we know today owes its structure, shape and amenities to the satisfaction of the needs of the visitor. To get a picture of the town in 1855 it is worth an extensive quotation from the *Illustrated London News* of 15 September that year:

> Llandudno is a new and flourishing bathing town lying between two bays. The water of the bay is particularly clear and affords most excellent bathing, being quite free from marsh and alluvial deposits; add to which the Great Orme's Head which shelters the town from the north, imparts a peculiar salubrity to the air, besides furnishing beautifully varied mountain walks, and an endless field for the botanist, containing some plants which are not found in any other part of the kingdom. Great Orme's Head is celebrated for its copper works, which are of great antiquity, and Celtic

A parliament of Commissioners, *c.* 1880.

implements and weapons of copper have been found. The old church (dedicated to St Tudno) . . . is dilapidated and now in disuse, and a new church was erected about 16 years ago. It is in contemplation to erect a handsome new church. An Act has been obtained for improving the town including draining and water supply; and also for constructing a harbour (to be called St George's Harbour) and a railway from the Conway Station to the Holyhead line. . . . There are packets twice daily from Liverpool and Beaumaris and a commodious landing pier is about to be constructed. Public baths are being built, and the town, which is the property of Lord Mostyn, is rapidly increasing. . . .

If you were looking for an adjective to describe the motives and results of the planners of the town in the 1850s the one that springs to mind immediately is 'quality'. The planning of the town, the control of the execution of the plans and the end results were all of the highest quality. This was largely due to the appointment of a group of Improvement Commissioners, seen on the previous page, who made it their duty to oversee almost every aspect of the town's development.

The first fifty or so crucially formative years were under their admirable control until they handed over to the Urban Council in 1895. This heritage lasted for many years, and there was always a resistance to the demands of brash commercialism, which has blighted the environments in so many seaside resorts. Latterly, however, there has been, in the opinion of many, a loosening of the qualitative grip and there are things going on that would not be acceptable to the Commissioners. Successive councils have, over the past couple of decades, allowed things to slip with sad consequences for the town. This could have been caused by changes in the structure of local government, coupled with reduced financial powers. From seemingly small matters such as allowing the Victorian lamp posts to rust away, to larger matters like not intervening when the beautiful Pier Pavilion visibly deteriorated because its owner's negligence, cause people to question local political power. The disastrous fire, which destroyed the Pavilion completely, was an avoidable tragedy. Now, seven years later, the ghastly hole left by the conflagration stays to remind everyone of their loss. Brown sites all over the town are ignored while attention is paid instead to the despoiling of green sites which need preserving. The new North Wales Theatre, a jewel in Llandudno's crown, stands next to the unkempt Arcadia theatre, once much loved but now becoming an eyesore.

In 1954, the town celebrated its centenary with exhibitions, parades and pageants. It produced a brochure, and I quote:

Not only is Llandudno lovely but it is also gay with all the attractions usually found in larger resorts. Moreover Llandudno is never crowded, for visitors disperse themselves to the two shores, the town, the Happy Valley, The Great Orme, and on tours and cruises. With some 2,000 hotels and boarding houses capable of accommodating 60,000 visitors a week, it is not surprising that great importance is placed on providing first class entertainments. During the season there are first class resident summer shows at the Pier Pavilion, Arcadia, and the Grand Theatre. Sunday concerts with famous stars are given at the Pier Pavilion and the Odeon. There are also three cinemas, two ballrooms, the open-air concert party, rollerskating, the Pierhead Orchestra, the Town Band, motor boats, speedboats and steamers. Sports are well catered for with three excellent golf links, fishing, cricket, tennis, bowls, putting and miniature golf. Few resorts in the British Isles can offer such a variety of scenery, interest and entertainment as Llandudno, which provides a blend of holiday attractions to suit the most critical taste.

A similar brochure written today would present quite a different picture. Tourism has sustained Llandudno for about 150 years, with peaks and troughs of intensity. Presently, like most other British resorts, the industry faces an uncertain future and the town appears to be taking refuge in providing retirement homes and shopping facilities which are springing up on brown sites all over. There will be pages in this book that will be looked at with sadness by many people, but there are so many features of the town and its location that cannot, and should not, be changed that hope must 'spring eternal'. Our Victorian and Edwardian forebears left us a wonderful heritage, a beautiful town in a magnificent setting, and many people believe that the enhancement of the beauty of its natural environment, and the preservation of its unique heritage is the only way to assure Llandudno's future.

The Photograph as a Historical Source

Within a month or so of the publication of *A Century of Llandudno* in 1999 the author was offered an archive of photographs from an unknown source. The collection of outstanding pictures taken mainly in the mid- to late-nineteenth century had, with one or two exceptions, never been published before. The opportunity arises to publish the photographs now, along with others taken more recently to demonstrate changing features of a developing town.

The dictum that the camera never lies has clearly been proven wrong over the years. In 1917 two young Yorkshire girls created the Cottingley Fairy photographs out of cardboard cut-outs and jiggery-pokery. They were successful enough to fool many people, including Sir Arthur Conan Doyle who went to his grave in 1930 with his belief in fairies confirmed by the prank.

Modern-day computer technology makes it even more important that today's photographic evidence should be subjected to careful scrutiny. Photographs of the past can be fed into the computer and manipulated all too easily. With a few clicks of the mouse, and the appropriate program, anyone would be capable of producing a seemingly authentic photograph of the sinking of the *Titanic* in Llandudno Bay after it had been bombed by a Graf Zeppelin piloted by Marilyn Monroe. . . . Many of the photographs shown here have been computer manipulated, but only to remove the dirt, the scratches and the ravages engendered by 130 years of careless handling.

A further pictorial source has been the vast wealth of picture postcards taken over the years by various photographers working for local and national companies. The author and his son have taken the contemporary photographs, and many were donated by generous friends.

1

The Great Orme

This awe-inspiring promontory is a mile wide and stretches 2 miles out to sea. Its name is Gogarth to the native Welsh. Every square yard of the Orme is full of history. This is where the town really began. Prehistoric remains, copper mines, myth and legend, religion, communication and habitation are all part of the Great Orme's story. To top it all, views the equal of anywhere in Great Britain are available from Pen-y-Gogarth (the top of the Orme). A short walk from the usually crowded car park on the summit yields a feast for the eyes: the Carneddau range where Snowdonia cascades into the sea, Anglesey and Puffin Island, the lovely Conway Valley, and in the other direction Rhyl and the hills of Clwyd. On a clear day, and with the proper vantage point, Ireland and the Isle of Man are visible across the sea.

The cromlech on Great Orme.

Evidence of an earlier civilisation exists in the cromlech. This consists of four large stones about 3½ft high with a capstone 7½ft long and nearly 6ft wide in the widest part. It was formerly called Lletty-y-Filiast (the kennel of the greyhound bitch), a name frequently associated with cromlechs throughout Wales. Could the bitch have been a guard dog? The finding of human remains in some of these cromlechs leaves little doubt that they were places of sepulture for persons of some importance in the community. They were almost certainly constructed in the neolithic age (4,500 BP) and their covering of smaller stones and earth has been washed away through the ages. There is evidence of cromlechs elsewhere on the Orme, and it is known that during the construction of the Marine Drive several were destroyed. A long barrow was also cleared in the Vaughan Street area when the railway came to town. It seems that later burial ceremonies were marked by the erection of a great pile of stones, and one such cairn lies on the western edge of the Orme, enlarged by visitors over the ages. The photograph below shows that the Great Orme goat is no respecter of ancient monuments either.

View from Pen-y-Dinas.

At about the time that the Romans were occupied on the Orme allegedly extracting the copper riches from the mines, the inhabitants lived in round enclosures on the higher ground nearby. One such encampment, Pen-y-Dinas, overlooks the town in the vicinity of Happy Valley and Camera Hill near the modern ski slope. Evidence of habitation is difficult to see because of the overgrowth of bramble and thorn bushes. Close examination reveals the presence of an encircling wall and round depressions indicate the circular huts in which the inhabitants lived. In 1993 the Gwynedd Archaeological Trust surveyed the Pen-y-Dinas and Great Orme area and found over 200 archaeologically interesting features and concluded that there were as many as 50 or 60 hut circles here. The photograph, right, taken by Tom Parry, shows a hut circle that was cleared of scrub in the late 1980s. Very little trouble and hardly any expense would make this site accessible as a tourist attraction.

Pen-y-Dinas Iron-Age hut circle.

Thomas Kendrick was born in Llandudno and christened in the Ebenezer Calvinistic Methodist church on 2 Dec 1821 as Thomas Cynric. The family lived at Craigside, but after the death of his father they moved to Ysceifiog in Flintshire. Sometime before 1842 Thomas and his brother were back in Llandudno working in the copper mines. They lived just below the famous cave at No. 4 Tan-y-Ogof ('below the cave'). Kendrick taught himself the stone-polisher's art, and combed the beaches looking for pebbles to polish and sell to the tourists. He moved into the cave and adapted it as both a home and a workshop. During his alterations he came upon ancient bones which he displayed outside the cave as a tourist attraction. The bones earned the serious attention of knowledgeable historians who were thrilled by the age of the finds and enthusiastically credited the site with authenticity, and the legend of Kendrick's Cave was born. Thomas Kendrick died aged 76 on Boxing Day 1897. From his humble origins he died a rich man, leaving £436 10*d* (£120,000 today's equivalent). The cave passed into the hands of the Humphreys family and has been preserved by them since Kendrick's death. It is still a site of international importance, and its glass frontage can be seen on the cliffs from the top of Mostyn Street to the right of the Empire Hotel. It is privately owned and on private land so trespassers are not welcomed without prior permission. His family still lives in Llandudno, and is rightly proud of their forebear.

The entrance to Kendrick's cave, 2001.

The photographs shown here were taken sometime in the last quarter of the nineteenth century and are of the bones allegedly found by Kendrick in his cave. They have been dated 14,000 BP, 12,000 BP and 5,9000 BP. Four other sites on the Orme have yielded bones of human origin. Ingram in 1885 listed Kendrick's bones as follows: 'fragments of human skeleton of individuals average height 5ft 6in (tibias embedded *in situ*), a considerable quantity of decorated swines' teeth holed to make a necklace, several bears' teeth drilled and decorated to make earrings, two lower equine jaws with inscribed patterns and highly polished incisors probably hung from the neck as ornaments'. Questions have been asked as to whether Kendrick found all of the bones on the one site in his cave, or whether the collection is a gathering together of finds made over the years as he explored the Orme, or from his years as a copper miner. Not all of Kendrick's finds have been accounted for, and it is believed that he was responsible for finding more than he is credited with. Some of the bones from the cave can be seen in the Copper Mine Museum on the Great Orme, some are in the British Museum in London. A Dr Dally of Birmingham offered to sell Mostyn Estates some bones from the collection before the First World War, but they did not purchase them. It is believed that a museum in Derbyshire received bones. Local reports also suggest that Kendrick sold bones and other artefacts to visiting Victorian amateur antiquarians. So, in

summary, they could be anywhere. Later in life he was involved with the running of the Camera Obscura on Camera Hill (see later) and in 1888 it is reported that he was responsible for a find of seventeen Roman coins and a piece of pottery while doing some road repairs near the Obscura.

Maes-y-Fachrell, Great Orme, *c.* 1912. In the Bronze Age a settlement was built on the Orme to extract and smelt the contents of the mineral rich veins, principally copper, which was exported far and wide throughout Europe. Recent findings (March 2002) suggest that at the same time as Stonehenge was being built, and long before King 'Tut' was buried, copper was being extracted from the mines on the Orme. This is one of the oldest, and certainly the most accessible ancient mine in Europe. The finding of 4,000-year-old scrapers made of animal bone in 1987 and 2002 excavations caused worldwide interest. These were not surface findings but came from holes 200ft into the mine. Getting the ore out was greatly facilitated by the fact that a natural chemical process which softened the rock (dolomitisation) made it easy to extract the ore with the primitive tools available during the Bronze Age – it is the only site in Great Britain where this is possible.

In the photograph above looking over the trams and in the middle distance is a part of the Great Orme known as Maes-y-Fachrell. The round shaft seen between the power posts is where the Vivyan shaft once was. This area is now developed as the Great Orme Copper Mine Complex (see over) and has achieved worldwide fame and won many awards as a visitors' attraction. A search for the origin of the name 'Maes-y-Fachrell' offers interesting and confusing historical information: 1. The field of the Mackerel – the place where the early inhabitants dried their fish. 2. A mutation of 'Maes-y-Fagwyr Allt' – literally 'the field of the fortified hill' – Iron Age origin perhaps. 3. A corruption of Welsh 'Macrell' – the name given the Roman Emperor Marcellus who was once in North Wales, 4. A mutation of 'Maes-y-Fach Arall', literally 'the field of the other little one', arising, who knows, from a disputed legacy in the past?

It is a sad fact that, for many years, the historical significance and importance of the Great Orme's mines was ignored. The desire to prettify the Orme in response to demands from the tourist industry led to a lot of its industrial heritage – buildings, washing floors, spoil heaps, etc. – being levelled, with a resulting loss of valuable archaeological data. The recent attempts by dedicated local historians and archaeologists to preserve what is left, and to uncover what was levelled, is bearing ripe fruits for the tourist industry and underlining the international importance of the area.

Copper mine workings, 2001.

The twenty years between 1830 and 1850 were high days of copper production in Llandudno. One problem facing the early owners was transport. The railway did not connect Llandudno with the Holyhead Line until 1858, and overland transport on poor roads was out of the question. The sea was the obvious highway for the export of ore, and the import of building material for the rapidly developing town. Ore was exported to Liverpool, Ravenshead, and Amlwch in the early years, but later the bulk of the ore went to Swansea for smelting. Boats of all descriptions, usually flat-bottomed, would sail in and beach on the North or West Shore. Carrying up to 90 tons, they were loaded from horse-drawn carts which carried the ore from the warehouses. Loading usually meant extra income for the miners and their families.

North Shore, the 'flats', *c.* 1880.

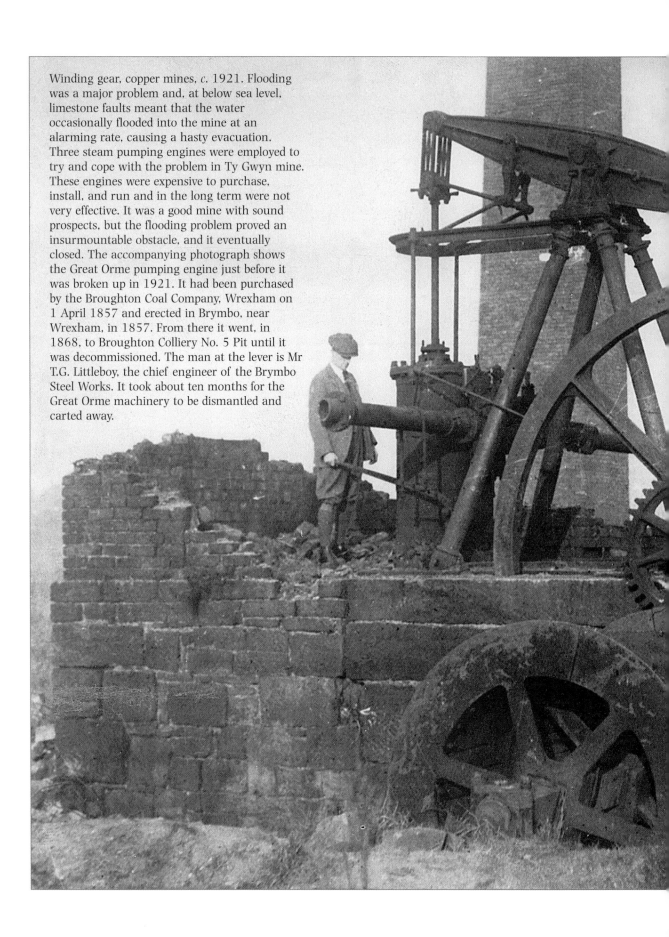

Winding gear, copper mines, *c.* 1921. Flooding was a major problem and, at below sea level, limestone faults meant that the water occasionally flooded into the mine at an alarming rate, causing a hasty evacuation. Three steam pumping engines were employed to try and cope with the problem in Ty Gwyn mine. These engines were expensive to purchase, install, and run and in the long term were not very effective. It was a good mine with sound prospects, but the flooding problem proved an insurmountable obstacle, and it eventually closed. The accompanying photograph shows the Great Orme pumping engine just before it was broken up in 1921. It had been purchased by the Broughton Coal Company, Wrexham on 1 April 1857 and erected in Brymbo, near Wrexham, in 1857. From there it went, in 1868, to Broughton Colliery No. 5 Pit until it was decommissioned. The man at the lever is Mr T.G. Littleboy, the chief engineer of the Brymbo Steel Works. It took about ten months for the Great Orme machinery to be dismantled and carted away.

On Pen-y-Dinas there is a rocking stone overlooking some precipitous cliffs. They have been called Logan Stones, and are said to have been transported by ice, and poised nicely on a pivotal rock as the ice receded. Some may have had the pivot enhanced at some time by a judicious blow from a hammer. The stone on the Orme has a plaque on it so it is easy to find, but not so easy to rock. Some believe that the powerful Druids meted rough ancient religious justice here, as they imbued these stranded boulders with magical and mysterious properties. Legend has it that this was the point at which criminals met the Druid elders for trial. If the case was too complicated for resolution by the elders, the miscreant was blindfolded and stood on the rock, and if it rocked he was innocent, if it didn't then he was guilty. The guilty party would be pitched over the nearby cliff, never to transgress Druidic law again. Another legend about this stone is that it was used as a pulpit or altar by St Tudno from which he conducted religious services.

Bishop's Palace, *c.* 1880. These ruins are situated near the shoreline on the south-western side of the Great Orme headland. Bishop Anian of the Diocese of Bangor officiated at the christening of Edward I's son, the future Edward II, at Caernarfon shortly after the conquest of 1282, and, by way of thanks, was granted the Manor of Gogarth. Sadly, most of what was built then was washed away by the sea or destroyed by fire when Owain Glyndwr famously rebelled in the fifteenth century. Its ruined state was the cause of a comment by Leland who visited the area in 1536, and said the palace was 'almost clene down'. It is believed that the site was well inland at the time of its construction, with several fields separating it from the shoreline. In 1891 the church sold the ruins and surrounding lands, and they now stand in the grounds of the Old Abbey Home. There was a mill in the palace grounds in the thirteenth century and the Palace and mill were valued at £4 1*s* 8*d* per annum in 1291. A later survey in 1352 by the Black Prince said that if the mill had been complete it would have been worth 4*s* but since it was in a state of disrepair it was worth only 2*s*. In 1088 it is recorded that Robert of Rhuddlan, a Norman leader, met his maker at the hands of Griffith ap Cynan under the cliffs of the Great Orme's Head. While Robert was enjoying an after-lunch siesta at Deganwy Griffith landed and filled his ships with Robert's cattle. Robert foolishly, but bravely, took on the Welshmen with the help of only one retainer. He fought 'like a wild boar', it is said, even though he had been pierced by many Welsh spears. Griffith sailed off with Robert's head nailed to his mast, and then to provoke the pursuing Normans he flung it into the sea before making off at great haste.

Monks' Path, 2001. This path will remain green throughout the longest drought, so the story goes, and the reason is that it has been blessed by the passage of so many holy feet over the centuries. It is supposed to be the route taken by the monks from the Bishop's Palace as they traversed the Orme on their way to St Tudno's church. The fact that it is also the route to the summit taken by thousands of sheep over the centuries tends to spoil the story. Before the Victorian era the route was known as Ffordd Las ('the green path'), and the name 'Monks' Path' is probably a name given in the nineteenth century to imbue the path with a spurious historical significance for the delectation of the visiting Victorian amateur antiquarians. From this path there is splendid view over the Conway Estuary to the coast where Snowdonia tumbles into the sea. If you take this walk, pause halfway and sit: allow your imagination to merge with mythology and mix with it some unproven theories. Daydream a while, and see a splendid palace rising out of the sea. You are looking at Llys Helig.

Llys Helig is the name given to some seaweed covered stones arranged in, more or less, straight lines which can be seen only when the tide is at its lowest about a mile off the coast at Penmaenmawr. This, some believe, is the site of the palace of Helig ap Glannog whose lands were swamped and lost for ever during a great flood sometime in the sixth century (give or take a century or two according to what your sources are!). In 1940 the Llandudno, Colwyn Bay & District Field Club published a fascinating account of an enquiry into the legend. The author, F.J. North DSc, FGS concludes that there is no evidence that the rock distribution is anything other than a natural formation left by a retreating glacier, the hand of man having little or nothing to do with it. There are those who prefer to believe the legend.

St Tudno's church, 1912.

Many of the towns and villages of Wales have their origins in small Christian settlements, and the 'llan' in their names refers to these origins: the word means the area in the proximity of a church or religious settlement. The second part of the place name refers usually to the saint with whom the Christian settlement is associated. In Llandudno's case the saint was St Tudno; the 't' is mutated to a 'd' to accord with a Welsh grammatical construction. St Tudno took up residence on the Great Orme sometime in the sixth century, choosing the site partly because it provided a good defensive outlook against seaborne invaders. Nothing of the original St Tudno's church has survived since it was probably constructed of easily degradable wattle and daub. In the twelfth century these wooden churches were rebuilt of stone, and the earliest remains of the St Tudno church dates back to this time. Over the years the building, subjected to punishing gales and storms from the sea, has been repaired and rebuilt. In 1855 after severe structural damage caused by years of neglect and a particularly violent storm the church was extensively repaired. Originally a community of Christian brothers probably lived here and there is evidence of farming activity close to the church. Field patterns and strip ploughing suggests that the area had been chosen because there was a modicum of shelter and reasonably flat cultivatable land nearby.

St Tudno's Church, 1924.

Happy Valley and Cust's Path, *c.* 1879. A journey on foot around the Orme at one time was the experience of a lifetime. Though the peninsula is criss-crossed by paths and primitive roads, a walk around its edge was perilous.

In the two years between 1856 and 1858 a London barrister and Trustee of Mostyn Estates, Reginald Cust, decided to build a path to make the journey less hazardous and more attractive to the growing numbers of visitors to the town. This was known, obviously, as Cust's Path. There was a charge of 1*d* to complete the walk, which provided for the path's upkeep. It is reported that Prime Minister Gladstone completed it in 1868 while on a visit to his friend Dean Liddell. The journey was so vertiginous in parts that he had to be blindfolded and led along by hand with the Liddell children walking along between him, the cliffs, and sea. The photograph above shows Cust's Path leaving the Happy Valley. A magnifying glass reveals plenty of interest in the central group: a man is roofing a building, there is a large telescope on a tripod, and a lady appears to be flexing her muscles with a bow and arrow (archery contests were held in the Happy Valley at one time). The valley itself appears to have only recently progressed from its quarry status. Right, a top hatted Victorian gent takes his ease at the side of the path, *c.* 1880.

Cutting the first sod of the Marine Drive development, 1878. In 1872 The Great Orme's Head Marine Drive Co. Ltd instigated a £14,000 building of Cust's Path, turning it into the present roadway known as the Marine Drive. The road was not completed until 1878 and it was reported, shamefully, that in the process of construction they cut through an Iron Age site and destroyed several burial chambers. As usual there were charges to use the road and these, in part, still exist, though greatly inflated. In 1878 pedestrians paid 1*d*, cyclists 2*d*, saddle horses 3*d*, carriages 6*d* per horse. Conway Borough Council now controls the road, and they charge for motor vehicles.

The Nose of the Orme, *c.* 1910.

Semaphore station, Great Orme, right *c.* 1875 and below, 1850s engraving. The semaphore system, once located on the summit of the Orme, was an arrangement of poles with extended arms that could be moved about, coupled with a flag pole on which Navy-style flag messages could be displayed. The station on the Orme was built in 1827 and extended in 1841. Within a decade of its extension the arms and flags were replaced by electricity and Morse code communication. It was not long before the station was dismantled and incorporated in the new summit complex that was being constructed. The semaphore

building was part of a visual chain which stretched from Holyhead to Liverpool, and its nearest neighbour was Puffin Island. A message could be relayed from one end of the system to the other in about four minutes, slightly faster than modern-day telephonic communication!

The Summit Hotel and complex replaced the semaphore station in 1909. It was built as a nine-bedroomed hotel. There was a golf course adjoining with 18 spectacular and exacting holes; this has now gone. In the Second World War it became a part of coastal defences when it was requisitioned by the RAF. In 1952 two men bought it, one of them being the middleweight champion of the world, Randolph Turpin. Turpin held the tenancy until 1961 when financial problems led to his selling it to Llandudno Council. His sad life came to an end in 1966 when he shot himself.

Summit complex, 2001.

Throughout the centuries the Ormes heads have been littered with the wrecks of unguided ships that have come to sudden and tragic ends on its cliffs. The history of the area is replete with tales of wreck plundering. The need for a lighthouse was apparent, but it was not until 1862 that one was built by the Mersey Docks and Harbour Board. The castellated fortress-like building stands imposingly on the cliff edge and was run by Trinity House until its time ran out on 2 April 1973. Every twelve seconds its 18,500-candlepower lamp flashed a signal which reached a distance of 24 miles out to sea. When atmospheric conditions were suitable it could be seen from Snaefell on the Isle of Man, a distance of 54 miles. The building, very sympathetically converted, is now a guesthouse with amazing sea views, and is currently up for sale at £825,000. The lamp still flashes for a distance of a few feet, but only on command, in the Great Orme Visitors' Centre, which must be visited.

La Marguerite passing the Great Orme lighthouse, *c.* 1908.

The Great Orme Exploration Society concerns itself with the study and preservation of all aspects of life on the Orme. Of current concern is the future of the Great Orme goats, a feral herd that has been roaming its slopes since the latter half of the nineteenth century. The progenitors of the present herd came from Kashmir, and were supposed to have been presented to Queen Victoria by the Shah of Persia shortly after her coronation. Research by Eve Parry, reported in her delightful little book, *Aliens on the Great Orme*, suggests, however, that they came from a herd brought into the country from France by Squire Christopher Tower of Brentwood, Essex in the early part of the nineteenth century. He presented a breeding pair to George IV who had been impressed by a Kashmir shawl that the Squire had produced. This was the start of the Windsor herd. In 1860 some breeding pairs were presented to Sir Savage Mostyn, and he released them on the Orme after breeding them at Gloddaeth Hall. They occasionally wreak havoc in gardens on the Orme, and there are demands for culling and sterilisation programmes to control them. In February 1990 twenty-six of the goats were moved to Hereford and the island of Flatholm. The resulting outcry at the unsympathetic way Aberconwy Borough Council had handled the situation shocked even them. The welfare of these goats should be of paramount concern in a town that is losing so much of its heritage to bungled and bumbling bureaucracy. A contraceptive programme (hormone implantation) is currently being carried out in an attempt to control these fascinating creatures.

Black Kashmiri goat, Great Orme (1999). Through the years a form of apartheid has been carried out on the slopes of the Orme. White Kashmiri goats occasionally produce black offspring and, in the past, whenever this has happened, the black kids were, to put it gently, disposed of by Mostyn Estates to preserve the purity of the herd. This practice, thankfully, has now ceased and a couple of black goats appeared four years ago, and we see one of them here, photographed by Tom Parry. This genetic throwback surprised everyone. Over the years the Great Orme goats have developed differences from the herd at Windsor. They are heavier, less shaggy and their horns are longer and bulkier. They have also developed a distinct antipathy to being caught and used as mascots by the Royal Welch Fusiliers.

Two RWF mascots.

Donkey boy with water pannier (*c.* 1910). There is a lack of surface water on the upper reaches of the Great Orme, because of the extreme porosity of the limestone rock. Water soaks through the upper strata and appears as springs lower down the headland where the limestone meets harder and older rock seams. Because of this, the inhabitants of the houses on the headland relied on the water-boy to provide their drinking supplies. Water Street on the Great Orme is so-called because of an ancient well and the steam pump that was situated here which pumped water into a reservoir in the Happy Valley. In 1798 Revd J. Evans, in his *Tour Through Wales* wrote, 'This village is small and ill-built, and in hot weather the springs which supply the inhabitants with water run dry, and they have to resort to the brackish wells in the marsh below.' It would appear that things had not changed much by 1910.

Right, the donkey boy is working as a carrier with his panniered animal.

Catering for tourists became a valuable source of income for the struggling sheep farms on the Orme. Farming here was always a difficult occupation with small financial rewards. Above is an early photograph of the Pink Farm Café. A later photograph shows the farm with a sign over the door which reads, 'Mrs J Roberts (Late) William Owen, Farm Inn, Great Orme's Head, licensed to sell Ale and Porter, Wines, Refreshments, etc.' The consumption of alcoholic drink in an area surrounded by precipitous cliffs would appear to be a little irresponsible.

The farm below is Penymynydd Isa, 'The White Farm', a single-storey structure which also tried to keep the wolf from the door by selling refreshments.

Presentation to the town of 'Happy Valley', August 1890. Happy Valley had originally been a limestone quarry which was closed in 1887 by the third Baron Mostyn. Work was carried out, so that by 1890 it was described as 'a charming natural amphitheatre on the Great Orme's Head, where a large concourse of pleasure seekers meet daily during the season'. Lord Mostyn conducted the opening ceremony and a drinking fountain was presented by his mother, Lady Augusta Mostyn. Mr Elias Jones, the chairman of the Improvement Commissioners, in his speech told the crowd that the daughter of a visitor, a Mr C.R. Hall, had first used the name 'Happy Valley' in 1855. Lord Mostyn in his reply to the speeches of thanks said, 'Standing on this romantic spot, I cannot help thinking of what Llandudno was twenty years ago. At that time there was neither pier, marine drive, nor splendid Promenade. There is little doubt that nature had done much for Llandudno, but at the same time the residents assisted by the Commissioners have done their duty in utilising and making the most of nature's gifts.' This sentiment needs reaffirming and acting upon today.

This delightfully peaceful garden area was once full of the dust, smoke and noise of a limestone quarry. At the end of the nineteenth century the area was more crowded than any other part of the town as it offered endless facilities for entertainment. The concert parties, brass bands, archery contests, the Camera Obscura, the beautiful rock gardens, country walks, greensward and pier all made the valley a centre of attraction, although the concert party seen above does not appear to have drawn a large crowd on this day. Below, we see a revivalist meeting, a children's special service mission conducted by Messrs Speers, Tyler and Bush (?) sometime around 1887.

Evidence of quarry work has disappeared so that the Valley is now a place to sit and relax. There is a lovely rock garden at the rear of the valley which consists of rocks brought in 1896 for the Eisteddfod that was held in that year. The large boulders set in the lawn were placed there in 1962 for the Gorsedd (bard-crowning) ceremony which took place for the 1963 Eisteddfod.

Haulfre Gardens, *c.* 1938. The name of the gardens means 'sun spot' and their situation on the south side of the Great Orme means that they do indeed receive plenty of sun. Nowadays they could do with a little more TLC. The gardens were designed and developed between 1871 and 1876 by the owner of the property, Henry Pochin, who went on to create the famous Bodnant Gardens in the Conway Valley, a Mecca for plant and garden lovers from all over the world. There is a splendid walk, with unforgettable views, from Haulfre Gardens towards the West Shore known as 'Invalids Walk'.

The view above of the modern Camera Obscura shows the structure built by a local man anxious to preserve a tradition which had been destroyed by vandals in 1966. Every view of this part of the town shows the Obscura perched on the hill behind the Grand Hotel. Lot Williams (left) had built the original in 1860 and the photograph shows him sitting outside the structure. He changed the panoramic views by climbing the ladder and moving the lens system by hand. Generations of tourists had enjoyed the views projected from its mirrors on to a white table in the darkened interior of the Obscura. At one time the earlier Obscura had been owned by Thomas Kendrick (see page 16).

Lot Williams and his Camera Obscura.

This is an old part of Llandudno with connections going back over seven hundred years. The building to the top right of the golf course is Wyddfyd Cottage built in the early part of the eighteenth century on the site of a building erected five centuries earlier. Before the area was enclosed there was an annual sheep fair here, and many of the early inhabitants combined the work of shepherd with that of miner. This pitch and putt course provided a picturesque wall with gentle exercise. Since the late 1980s more vigorous exercise now goes on in this valley, which has lost its beauty as a result. There is no question that the ski slope and toboggan run are welcome additions to a town lacking in holiday amenities, but some attention needs to be paid to making the area more visually attractive. A good landscape consultant would work wonders here. Road access to the slope is a little hair-raising and some more passing places would be welcomed.

Happy Valley Terminus for Great Orme Cabin Lift, 2001. Another 'longest and best' for Llandudno was the coming of the Cabin Lift in 1969. The tramway is the longest funicular (cable) railway in Great Britain, and the cable carries passengers from the Happy Valley to the Orme's summit with awe-inspiring views and not a little excitement all the way.

2

The Town Develops

When Owen Williams sat on the side of the Orme in 1846 and regarded its prospect towards the Little Orme 2 miles away he would have seen a stretch of marshy scrubland occupied mainly by sheep and cattle with a few cottages dotted about. At his feet would be the Old Village with its population of miners and fishermen living in relative poverty and scraping a hard living from shepherding, fishing and mining. The houses were clustered around what is now the Old Road in terraces on the slopes of the Orme. There was also the detritus of industrial activity, steam engines, pit shafts, a crushing mill, and piles of pit spoil. He envisaged the growth of a town using its position and beauty to become one of the new and burgeoning crop of seaside resorts which were springing up all over Britain. Ten years later and his dream is becoming reality, as shown in the lithograph above dated 1856.

Artist's sketch of The Creuddyn, 1849. On the Creuddyn itself there was a group of twenty-five or so cottages dotted about, mainly near the shoreline and in what is now the Church Walks and Mostyn Street area. These houses were known as *ty un nos* or *hafod un nos* meaning 'one-night-house'. According to an old Welsh custom if a house could be constructed in one night and have a fire burning in the hearth by morning then the builder was granted property rights. The freeholders cleared these from the prime spots as the town developed and the squatter occupants were housed in Madoc Street. The above drawing dated 1849 presents an artist's impression of the area.

This charming pen sketch shows a fisherman's cottage on what is now the Parade, dated 1851.

This view towards the Great Orme is from Pwllygwichiaid. The name means the 'pool of the periwinkles', and it was here in 1790 that Hugh Hughes, an artist and engraver of great talent, was born. South Parade on the Promenade is on land that once belonged to Pwllygwichiaid.

This lively engraving of 1858 is entitled Llewelyn Street (Llewelyn Avenue) and shows the housing development at the base of Old Road.

Tudor Street (Road) is shown in this engraving. The present Tudor Road links Mostyn Broadway with the Promenade. This gives a wider perspective and encompasses part of the West Shore, and it shows the buildings of Church Walks spreading along the flanks of the Orme towards Plas Gogarth, seen in the 1857 engraving below.

The lithograph above, of about 1858, shows the town development proceeding along the sea front with the beginnings of the row of hotels. Mostyn Street is beginning to take shape and assert itself as the town's main thoroughfare. We can see here the beginnings of the 'grid' structure which determined the layout of the town. The Llandudno planners used the Great Orme (Gloddaeth Street) and the North Shore (Promenade) to form the basis for the grid, with other streets conforming to the rectangular pattern inasmuch as the natural shape of the Creuddyn would allow.

In about 1860 photographers began to appear and depicted the environment with cameras rather than the engraver's needle. This, to some extent, removes artistic licence from the process and we begin to get truer pictures. This photograph (*c.* 1870) was taken from the Great Orme and shows the development of the town along the Promenade and across the Creuddyn. Centrally it is noticeable that Trinity Church is newly built and without its spire. In the middle distance Conway Road snakes out of the town, and this reference point is useful for the purpose of historical comparison. This road is now the A470, the major access route into the town, linking with the motorway system via the A55.

Opposite, above: A later photograph is from a picture postcard and was probably taken at the turn of the nineteenth century from Invalid's Walk. The feature to note here is that the town is, as it were, fattening out and developing across the fields towards the West Shore. Gloddaeth Street is unmetalled and empty, but St George's Hotel has its lift and water tower, seen in the distance against the sparkling waters of the bay.

Opposite, below: This aerial photograph from the 1930s shows the confined space within which the town developed, the area circumscribed by the Ormes and the two shores. Unfortunately in cloud-shadow, the development the other way from the Little Orme and Craig-y-Don is obscured.

The postcard above was mailed in 1933, and was taken from Fferm Bach, behind the North Wales Medical Centre in the foreground. It is a better and clearer view than on the previous page, of the development of Craig-y-Don, which occurred relatively late in the town's history.

An aerial view of the Creuddyn, taken after 1994 when the Pier Pavilion was lost, merits a good 'walk' with the eye. The town has changed little since this photograph was taken.

3

Pier, Promenade
& Beach

Between 1814 and 1910 a total of eighty-nine piers were built on the coast of England and Wales. Many were short-lived ventures and most underwent rebuilding programmes to repair storm, fire and other damage brought about by their vulnerable position.

The first pier built in Llandudno in 1858 was not, in fact, designed for the needs of the perambulating holidaymaker. The purpose was much more practical; it was built as part of Llandudno's abortive attempt to become an important industrial and packet boat port connecting mainland Britain with Ireland. For years rival claims for this highly lucrative postal contract had been causing controversy in North Wales. The principal contenders were Holyhead on Anglesey and Porth Dinllaen on the Lleyn Peninsula. An Orme's Bay proposal had been tendered in 1836, which included a line from the Grand Junction Railway through Chester to Orme's Bay. At this time the site of the future town was a waste of scrub, marsh and sand dunes. The outcome of the contest was decided when Anglesey's main stumbling block, the crossing of the Strait, was removed by the construction of Robert Stephenson's tubular bridge at Britannia Rock. It is not too difficult a feat of imagination to visualise Llandudno Bay as it would have been had the St George's Harbour and Railway Bill passed successfully through Parliament in 1837.

Llandudno's first pier had a very short life. It was built in 1858 and in 1859 on 26 October one of the worst storms in recorded history hit the Irish Sea and the coasts of Britain. It was in this storm that the Royal Charter, en route from Australia, came to grief off Moelfre with 459 lives lost. The coast of North Wales was littered with wrecks. Llandudno Pier came to grief, and it was reported that it was demolished soon afterwards because of the extent of the damage. Research by Diane and Nigel Bannerman (1999), however, suggests that in fact the pier was repaired and was used for several more years after the storm. Their suggestion seems to be backed up by photographic evidence as, for example, in the accompanying photograph. This was probably taken in the late 1860s or early 1870s, and close scrutiny shows a pier in the background, either under construction or the reverse.

Llandudno Pier was instrumental in ensuring the early economic viability of the town since it was the port of entry for many thousands of visitors from Liverpool and the Lancashire Coast. As described elsewhere, *La Marguerite* alone was capable of bringing in around a thousand visitors a day in the height of the season. On one day, 20 July 1907, the steamship company offloaded 3,181 passengers at the pierhead. The busy photograph above shows the pier with *La Marguerite* heading off to Liverpool and a smaller vessel, probably the *Snowdon*, arriving at the pier. This pier was built in 1877 with an additional spur in 1884.

Waiting for the steamer, *c.* 1902.

The pier, with The Grand Hotel in the background, *c.* 1928. John Betjeman wrote, 'A pier is about the only place left in any town where walking is possible without having to look back all the time for oncoming vehicles. It also provides a walk on the sea without the disadvantage of being seasick. In fact piers are havens of fresh air and freedom from anxiety which we can ill afford to lose.' The pier was also a place of entertainment and Llandudno, like so many other piers, had a diver, for what is a pier without a diver? Many will recall the wartime ITMA programme and the catchphrase 'Don't forget the diver Sir! Don't forget the diver!' Llandudno Pier had its diver in the early years of the twentieth century. He would take the plunge in handcuffs and emerge free. At night he completed the trick after setting fire to himself. Unfortunately no one has been able to come up with a photograph of this intrepid daredevil. He was known as Professor Beaumont. Fishing, alcohol, amusement arcades and penny-in-the-slot machines are the only entertainment on the pierhead now, replacing the lovely music of John Morava and the Pier Orchestra.

John Morava and the Llandudno Pier Orchestra, *c.* 1968.

Pier bandstand, *c.* 1880. This was the first bandstand on the pierhead, where Round's band would perform. A larger concert hall was built later (now an amusement arcade) and John Morava and the Pier Orchestra performed there from 1938 until 1974. The orchestra played for thirty-seven seasons and gave an estimated 10,000 concerts.

The 'end of the pier show', 2001.

The Baths Hotel. A conspicuous building in all of the early photographs and engravings of the town, the Baths Hotel started off in 1855 as the Baths Reading Room and Billiard Hall. In 1875, with the addition of a western annexe, it became the Baths Hotel. It was a place for the gentlemen and young bloods of the town, and, in the late 1870s, it was frequented by a Russian prince, a grand duke and a general who whiled away the time playing chess. A book published by Thomas Williams in 1864 speaks of the Baths as an ideal place for viewing rough seas and 'enraged elements' when the north-east wind blows. The building was demolished in 1900 to make way for the Grand Hotel. The largest swimming pool in Great Britain had been opened under the Pier Pavilion in 1884. This lasted sixteen years before the demolition materials from the Bath House filled it in.

The Bath House from Pen-y-Dinas, *c.* 1880.

LLANDUDNO

SUBSCRIPTION LIBRARY AND NEWS ROOM,

AT THE PUBLIC BATHS,

(WESTERN END OF THE MARINE PARADE.)

A SINGLE SUBSCRIPTION of 3s. a week, 5s. a fortnight, 8s. a month, 12s. two months, 16s. a quarter, £1 1s. the half year, or £1 11s. 6d. the year, allows one work at a time, and the use of the Reading Room to one person.

A DOUBLE SUBSCRIPTION of 5s. a week, 8s. a fortnight, 12s. a month, 18s. two months, £1 1s. a quarter, £1 10s. half a year, or £2 2s. a year, allows two works at a time, and the use of the Reading Room to two persons.

A FAMILY SUBSCRIPTION of 7s. a week, 10s. a fortnight, 15s. a month, £1 2s. two months, £1 10s. a quarter, £2 half a year, or £2 12s. 6d. a year, allows three works at a time, and the use of the Reading Room to three persons.

THE READING-ROOM

Is handsome and commodious, and is regularly supplied with the London Newspapers (by Express), the Provincial Journals, and the Magazines. It commands fine views of the sea and the mountains, and is elegantly furnished. New works are regularly added to the Library. Day Tickets of admission to the Reading Room, one shilling each. Books lent to read to parties who are not Subscribers to the Reading Room on special terms, which may be learned on application to the resident Librarian.

A PIANO-FORTE, for the use of Subscribers to the Room, at stated periods.

During the season there will be a series of CONCERTS and LITERARY ENTERTAINMENTS, of which due notice will be given.

* Rooms for Billiards and Chess.

De la Rue's Stationery, Guide Books, Views in Wales, and other Engravings, with an elegant variety of Fancy Articles, on Sale.

There are BATHS in the lower stories, where the Bath-keeper is in attendance : Ladies down the stair-case to the right hand—Gentlemen to the left. The use of Baths does not give the right of admission to the Reading Room, unless the party using them should be a Subscriber.

Once the largest hotel in Wales, the Grand replaced the Baths Hotel, seen earlier, in 1901. It had 156 bedrooms, and over the years many famous people have occupied them. Sir Winston Churchill stayed here in 1948, when the Conservative party held their annual conference in Llandudno. He slept in room 109. Later, in 1973, a fire started by an arsonist caused a considerable amount of very costly damage; sixteen days later he tried to start another fire but was apprehended and imprisoned for life. Sadly, in 1994, the Grand lost the building that complemented it architecturally, the Pier Pavilion, which people believe succumbed to another arsonist one fateful February night. The Grand Hotel itself was very close to being fire damaged during this disaster, and was saved only by the outstanding work of the North Wales Fire Service. The hotel has 169 bedrooms now and is owned by the National Grand Hotel Group.

The Grand Hotel and town from Pen-y-Dinas, 2001.

Pier Pavilion and Camera Hill, early twentieth century.

The Pier Pavilion, a beautiful listed building, did not deserve its eventual fate. Purchased and neglected by a private buyer it was subjected to a battering by the elements over the years and was slowly being destroyed. The building eventually succumbed to vandals and in February 1994 it was gutted by fire. A hundred years of history went in a few disastrous hours. In the *North Wales Weekly News* of 2 August 2001 there is an article which describes the ruins as a 'rat infested bombsite'. Mr Roy Gambrill, a town councillor, has been bombarding Conway County Council and the new Welsh Assembly with letters in an attempt to get something done. Either because of their ineptitude or their lack of interest, his commendable efforts seem to be getting nowhere. The owners are a Midlands-based company who claim that the insurance they received after the fire was not sufficient to rebuild the theatre and to date they have certainly not spent any of the money they received on improving the ghastly mess left. The site is now home to eight feral cats, being fed by an animal lover (bottom right). In March 2002 the council declared that they no longer know who the owners are so can do nothing. This statement was received with universal derisive disbelief.

Pier Pavilion site 2001.

PROMENADE

The initial attraction of the seaside was, of course, the sea and its health-giving properties. For best effect the 'waters' needed to be accompanied by gentle exercise and the intake of deep breaths of ozone. To this end most seaside resorts built Promenades for gentle strolling and the smooth transit of invalid carriages. Llandudno's Promenade, designed initially by Owen Williams before 1854, is a Promenade probably unequalled in the world. Walking it is unalloyed pleasure, and its character must be preserved at all costs. Williams, at a later date, said the initial design was criticised by the property developers of the day who, displaying the same lack of foresight as those of today, said it was a waste of valuable building space. His reply was: 'If I had had my own way it would have been deeper.' The 2-mile sweep of the Promenade is edged with seats, and sitting and staring into space is a lovely way to spend a couple of hours. No trading is allowed, and strident commercialism is held within the confines of the pier. The Promenade is all the better for it.

The promenade in the late 1960s.

Llandudno. Photograph by Jim Roberts.

It would be so easy for the beauty of the Promenade to be ruined by architectural follies and indiscriminate colour choices in hotel decoration, but this thankfully is controlled. As a result, the hotels add to the seafront's attraction. The view from the pier with the sweep of the bay and the well-kept hotels never fails to please the eye. There are one or two eyesores in this 2-mile stretch, for example, the Arcadia is submitting to, and being destroyed by, time, council neglect (they own it so they have no excuse), and the elements. And there is an ugly dirt patch alongside the North Wales Theatre, also owned by the council, which could do with some trees and flowers.

One character who did trade on the Promenade was the bathchair man, shown here. It was this man's job to transport invalids along the Promenade to ensure that they breathed in their fair share of fresh, ozone-enriched air. Early photographs frequently show a row of these chairs near the pier entrance. The 'man' was Jabez Hodgetts, who hailed from Birmingham. He was a jeweller by trade but moved to Llandudno to establish himself on the Promenade. He died, aged 72, in 1909, having worked in Llandudno for eight years. His great granddaughter, Mrs Dorothea Ruddle, who kindly loaned this photograph, lives in Craig-y-Don.

Bathchairs disappeared from the Promenade soon after the First World War.

St George's Hotel, Marine Parade. Following hard on the heels of the decision that Llandudno was to be a holiday resort, Isaiah Davies stepped in and built Llandudno's first 'grand' hotel. He was born in 1831 on the Great Orme. His business sense and entrepreneurial spirit led to a shrewd marriage with the daughter of the proprietor of the King's Head Inn. The young lady was much older than Isaiah and stood to inherit a good deal. The inn was left to Isaiah and his wife. None other than Lord Mostyn's land agent, one John Williams, was a frequent visitor to the inn.

A huge 'slate', it is alleged, was wiped clean when Isaiah was offered the choice of the building plots on what was to be the new Promenade. In 1855 Isaiah Davies at the ripe old age of 24 became the proud owner of Llandudno's first major seafront hotel, the St George's. Comparisons between the engraving and the present-day photograph will indicate the extent to which the building has been altered over the years. In 1878 it was extended towards Mostyn Street and the water tower was built so that Llandudno's first lift could be installed. In 1856 the first horse omnibus service to Conway railway station originated as, at that time, there was no rail link between Llandudno and the Chester–Holyhead line. There are many famous names associated with sojourns at this hotel: Bismarck, Disraeli, Gladstone, Lloyd George, Churchill, Napoleon III and his wife Eugenie all stayed here.

St George's Hotel, 2001.

The Marine Hotel. The story told of this hotel would have made a good libretto for a D'Oyly Carte opera production. In 1890, the Queen of Roumania, who wrote romantic novels under the name of Carmen Silva, was looking for somewhere to relax, a remote spot where she could recharge her creative batteries; a friend suggested Wales. When she alighted from her train she found herself in Llandudno, and the busy, bustling holiday resort was not at all what she had expected. She arrived with due ceremony at the Marine Hotel and stayed for five weeks, a period of time the town will never forget. Whenever she ventured out of doors she was followed by adoring crowds, numbering in the

The Imperial Hotel played host to another royal visitor just before the Second World War. She was the exiled Queen Rambai Barni of Siam. She was made to leave the hotel at the start of hostilities because the government had requisitioned it. It became the wartime headquarters of the Inland Revenue. Prior to 1872, the hotel had been a collection of smaller guesthouses which were amalgamated and extended with upper floors added. The top floor was gutted by fire in 1972 and an extensive building programme was required to restore it. Now, the hotel enjoys three-star status, and has 100 luxury bedrooms with a gymnasium, heated swimming pool and sauna. Many of its wartime inhabitants developed a warm affection for Llandudno and a high proportion of them came back to the town on retirement.

thousands, and she only had to step into a shop for a sign to appear the next day 'By Royal Appointment'. Some of the shopfront views in this book have this appellation. Two roads in Craig-y-Don were named in her honour 'Carmen Silva Road' and 'Roumania Drive'. To mark her departure, twenty-four lifeboat rockets were fired from the Great Orme. Despite the furore, the Queen is said to have remarked of the town that it was a 'Beautiful haven of peace'. This remark, translated into Welsh *Hardd, Hafan, Hedd*, has become the town's motto. For the rest of her life, as far as we know, she never visited nor mentioned the town again.

St Tudno's Hotel. This small hotel is of historical interest as well as being renowned for its very high standards. It was built very early in the history of the town in the 1850s. Thomas Jones, with his wife Eliza, opened the hotel and called it Tudno Village Lodging House. This was the first hotel to be associated with the Alice in Wonderland legend. The Liddell family with a large retinue of servants stayed here in 1861. Their second visit was to the St George's Hotel, and then they had a house built on the West Shore. The present hotel is of extraordinarily high standards and has won many prestigious awards including: 'Best Seaside Resort Hotel in Britain' and 'Which? Hotel Guide 'Hotel of the Year 1999'.

The 81-bedroomed Queen's Hotel was opened in 1855, hard on the heels of the first hotel on the Promenade. The area was considered to be so far away from the town at this time that its postal address was 'Near Llandudno'. St George's Crescent joins the Queen's Hotel with the St George's. The postbox outside should not be passed unnoticed as it is of great age; it is a few years short of being 140 years old and is still in use. This hotel has been owned and run by the same family for over twenty years.

THE QUEEN'S HOTEL,
Marine Parade, LLANDUDNO.

Distant on the London and North Weston Railway, one hour-and-a-quarter from Holyhead or Chester, and five-and-a-half-hours from London.

THIS Hotel has been recently enlarged and will be found replete with every comfort and convenience for Families and Tourists. *Arrangements made for Boarding by Week or Month.*

UNDER NEW MANAGEMENT,
For Tariff, &c., apply to the Manager.

Short for hydropathic, the Hydro Hotel (below) was opened in 1860 to provide water treatments. For the first twelve years of its existence, under the medical supervision of a Dr Norton, it didn't exactly prosper. In 1872 a practitioner from Caernarfon, Dr Henry Thomas, took over. His qualification (MD Homeopathic College of Pennsylvania 1855) was not recognised in England but, despite this, he continued to call himself a Doctor of Medicine until he died in 1894. In addition to the traditional water immersions and infusions he carried out many supposed curative techniques, most of which would be treated with derision nowadays.

Between the Arcadia and Craig-y-Don there is the rather unprepossessing building of the Llandudno Sailing Club. The first recorded activities of the club are dated at the end of the nineteenth century but this photograph taken at a club regatta is from *c.* 1907. The popularity of the event is easy to judge by the large crowd gathered to observe. The club possesses a trophy dated 1860 so it has a long history. The present clubhouse was built in 1968 some eight years after the present club was formed.

Sailing, 2001.

These happy holidaymakers are outside the Ormescliffe Hotel, a large comfortable hotel in the Craig-y-Don area, *c.* 1907. The interesting feature here is the building in the background jutting towards the Promenade. This was the original Washington Hotel, which protruded so far on to the road that it proved a traffic hazard and had to be demolished in 1925. The present Washington Hotel with its pleasing copper dome was built in the same year.

The County Hotel, *c.* 1910. The Davies family of snooker fame owned the County Hotel, formerly the Craig-y-Don boarding house, for many years. Fred Davies and his more famous world champion brother Joe gave exhibition matches there and attracted large crowds. A national coach company now owns the hotel and it is one of the busiest on the Promenade.

The Craigside Hydro stood majestically dominating the Little Orme side of the bay for almost eighty-six years. It was built in 1888 and demolished in 1974. My daughter thought of it as an enchanted castle during her childhood. As its name implies it was originally built to offer hydropathic treatment. The forecourt of the hotel provided excellent facilities for tennis, and across the road from the hotel were indoor courts of international standard. The area is now a highly desirable residential suburb overlooking the bay and the green fields of Bodafon.

Bodafon Fields model farm, 2001. Property developers and consortia are casting lustful eyes on Bodafon Fields ; they want to cover them with car parks, pleasure domes and high-cost housing. Some years ago, Mostyn Estates tried to build a Disney-style Alice in Wonderland theme park here in view of the Liddell family connection, but pressure from residents and the local authority put a stop to that. However, they keep coming back with other schemes and it is to be hoped that those who oppose them can match their obstinacy. The current proposal is to concrete the field in order to provide a massive car park for a Park and Ride scheme. Many regard this as the thin end of a wedge which will lead to wholesale house building and the permanent loss of yet another of Llandudno's attractive and irreplaceable features.

THE BEACH

An early, crowded beach scene at Llandudno shows clearly the Victorian and Edwardian antipathy to sun worship. The children and ladies, there are no men present, are well protected from the sun's harmful rays, and the two girls centre right have their faces shielded by hooded bonnets. The fear is not of any adverse medical condition that might be caused, but of becoming coarsely brown and looking like a member of the working class. Beauty in those days was marked by a pallid languor, and rosy cheeks were characteristic of the peasant. The lad in the foreground is clearly out of his class; he is one of Llandudno's urchins who has wandered into the photograph. His clogs and clothing set him apart from the rest: he is probably a 'donkey boy'. The absence of men except for one or two on the Promenade in the background suggests that this is the segregated Ladies' Bathing Beach.

The two photographs on this page repay close scrutiny. The main picture is of particular interest and is a very early beach view, from sometime in the 1860s or '70s. The Bathhouse (built 1855) is without its annexe, which was added in 1875, and the pier is what remains of the one destroyed in 1859. There are only a few bathing machines; later photographs usually show a row of them rimming the sea's edge. The picture below is post-1900 and shows the significant changes that can occur in the space of a decade or so. The Grand Hotel (1901) and the Pier Pavilion (1886) have supplanted the Bath House, and the pier (1877) has been replaced by the present structure.

In the early days, naked bathing was common among men while ladies wore all-encompassing bathing dresses. A tourist in North Wales, writing in 1795, was aghast at the nude bathing antics of the 'inferior orders of people' who 'commonly bathe without the usual precautions of machines and dresses'. In 1868 the Improvement Commissioners passed a law forbidding nude bathing and introduced single-sex bathing areas with a 150-yard gap between them. It became an offence punishable by a heavy fine for a man to go into the sea without either a bathing apron or drawers. Bathing machines had been on the beach for fifteen years by this time. Segregated bathing was in force until 1894 when the council passed a by-law allowing mixed bathing in the sea off the beach adjoining the Arcadia, provided the bathers were attired appropriately. From 1855 machine operators were obliged to provide bathing dresses for ladies but not for men. It was clear that this system did not work very well, largely because no-one wanted to wear other people's unsavoury cast-offs. In the photograph below, taken in about 1920, bathers are no longer relying on the machines for privacy. The Llandudno machines, however, remained part of the beach furniture into the 1950s.

Bathing machines, *c.* 1912. Wheeled horse-drawn sheds were already in use in the mid-eighteenth century, and appear frequently in early beach photographs. The shed was designed to deter the voyeur and the poseur since it removed the need for a lady to walk across the beach in a state of *deshabillé*. She would enter the machine while on dry land and during the bumpy and bruising trip to the sea would undress and don her bathing dress, and then, when finished, she would appear out of the hut safely far from prying eyes. In Margate an enterprising gent perfected the modesty umbrella. At an appropriate depth a telescopic awning would be released into the sea creating a small space away from watchers, the burning sun and the prevailing breeze. In this enclosure the lady performed her ablutions, 'in a manner consistent with the most refined delicacy'.

Bathing near the Pier, 2001. Sea- and sunbathing, formerly such a popular part of the holiday scene, are on the decline. Although Llandudno's beaches have usually been given a clean bill of health by the beach inspectors, bathers and swimmers are now a rarity. The reasons are obvious. Compared with Mediterranean seas there is a distinct temperature difference. There is no longer the belief in the magical curative powers of sea bathing. Horror stories about sea pollution are common, and the folly of lying in direct sunlight with its life-threatening ramifications is now universally accepted. There is also a reason of particular significance to Llandudno. Bathers and paddlers like a sandy beach and this they will find on the less popular beach at the West Shore. The popular North Shore, which was a mixture of pebble and sand areas, has been changed in the past few years. Fears about coastal erosion in the 1990s led to most of the pebble beach being covered with thousands of tons of rough hewn rock, very uncomfortable to walk on. Only a small part of the extensive beach was left suitable for traditional children's activities. Some considered this an excessive response to the problem, but something had to be done or the beach might have been washed away forever, along with the Promenade.

Elizabeth Hughes, donkey lady, *c.* 1879.

For children at the seaside, the pleasures are traditional and unchanging: digging in the sand, building castles, burying Dad, paddling and riding on the donkey. Donkeys arrived at the seaside some time in the late eighteenth century, probably introduced by gypsies so that Victorian and Edwardian ladies might be transported without too much effort along the beaches and Promenades. In David Copperfield the redoubtable Betsy Trotwood was in constant conflict with the donkeys that passed her cottage on the cliffs. The precise date of their introduction to Llandudno's beaches is difficult to discover, but an estimate of 1870 would not be far out. The photograph above dates from this very early time. Several families were involved in the trade, among them the Hugheses, the Dunns, the Winstanleys and the Davis family. The Hughes family were among the first and the line continues to this day with Mrs Burroughs, the great niece of Elizabeth Hughes, still carrying on the business. The families traded from the lifeboat slipway, radiating out from its base as tidal conditions allowed. One trader, Billy Pip, sold his business to the Jones family in the

early 1940s. Les Jones came out of the army in 1945 and used his gratuity to buy into his father's business. From the end of the Second World War two families dominated the trade: the Joneses and Hugheses. Mrs Burroughs (left), the elder daughter of Llew Hughes, still provides rides along with Mr and Mrs Les Jones. They each run a string of about twelve donkeys, and, by amicable agreement, take it in turns to operate from the more favourable side of the slipway on a daily basis. John Jones is to take over the business eventually, so continuity is guaranteed.

Mrs Burroughs with charges, 2001.

At one time it was possible to hire a sailing or rowing boat on the beach. The rows of boats on the shore here are for hire. The Improvement Commissioners set up a series of laws and by-laws for their regulation, these laws imposed a heavy fine for any boatman who overcharged or who did not make every arrangement for the comfort of the hirers. The boats were to be numbered and kept in proper repair. The charges were: 'For a whole boat for a time not exceeding one hour – 2s. And for the first half hour afterwards – 1s.'

Sailing boats, c. 1918.

A trip around the bay on the *White Heather* on this day is of particular significance because it includes a cruise around the battleship *Iron Duke* which is on a courtesy visit to the town. For a *2s* fee you are offered a close-up view of this magnificent flagship of the King's fleet. The date of the photograph would be about 1920. Trips around the Bay with unforgettable views of the Orme from the sea are on offer today, and an additional attraction this year is a thrilling turn on a speedboat.

Boat trippers, 2001.

WEST SHORE

Taken not long after the completion of the construction of the Marine Drive, this early photograph shows the West Shore exit tollgate. The road is as yet unmetalled. There is a wonderful panoramic view from this shore which takes in the Conway estuary, Penmaenmawr Mountains, the opening to the Menai Strait, Anglesey and Puffin Island. The sunsets are breathtaking. Dean Liddell and his wife (Alice in Wonderland's parents) honeymooned in North Wales in 1846, and they fell in love with its wild splendour. In 1859 they visited Penmaenmawr's most famous tourist, William Ewart Gladstone, who had been the Dean's friend since their university days together. The Liddells came to Llandudno for the day, and the burgeoning town took their fancy. Their next holiday was during Easter 1861 when they stayed at the Tudno Villa (now the St Tudno Hotel, North Parade).

Miners' cottages, c. 1920. As early as 1783 buildings were appearing in the dunes of Penmorfa (West Shore). Twelve single-storey cottages were built to house the copper miners who were working in the mines owned by the Mostyn family and the Bishop of Bangor. A terrace of these houses is seen on all photographs taken of the West Shore until 1936 when they were demolished. They had a life of over 150 years. This area was, in fact, a hive of mining activity with a river of fresh water running out of the side of the Orme, which drained the mine workings. This can still be seen in Abbey Place. The water proves useful in that it supplies water for the model yacht pool seen on page 78.

Cottage demolition, 1936.

Gogarth Abbey Hotel, *c.* 1930. The Liddells decided to build a home in the town, and they chose the wild and desolate, though spectacular, West Shore as the site. They returned to Oxford with all the arrangements made and in the summer of 1861 they came back to Llandudno and stayed at St George's Hotel with their large family and their entourage of servants. There were problems of course, tardy builders and West Shore sewerage among them, and it was not until 16 August 1862 that they moved in. They had many holidays here spasmodically throughout the next nine years, and then Dean Liddell sold the property to an Oxford friend. The four-storey section of this building with the bay and dormer windows is the original Pen Morfa. This has been added to and modified over the years to make the Gogarth Abbey Hotel the splendid hotel it is today.

It is believed, with little evidence, that Lewis Carroll visited the Liddells in Pen Morfa. The environment and young Alice Liddell is said to have inspired him to write his world-renowned books. A memorial commemorating this event was unveiled on the West Shore in 1993. Persistent vandalism caused the council to cage the memorial and surround it with a moat. The statue has been in a damaged condition for the past twenty years or so and no attempts have been made by the council to repair it.

A group of enthusiasts pose for the camera at the edge of the model yacht pool, in the late nineteenth century. They took this hobby so seriously that they even dressed like yachtsmen of the day. The beautifully crafted boats were probably handmade. The men are locals, not tourists and among them are: John Davis, John Evans, Ivor Davis, James Griffiths, and Gwylim Jones. The water is fresh and supplied in a constant stream from the nearby mine workings. Recent attempts to bring model boating back as a hobby met with no success; nor did proposals to introduce further tourist and leisure attractions to the area.

Golfing at Maesdu, *c*. 1920. Llandudno boasts two fine golf courses within its confines and there are several more within striking distance. One of the town's major courses is Maesdu ('the Black Field') on the site of the famous Battle of Deganwy, AD 1098. In 1915 the first municipal golf course in Wales was built here. The original design was by Harry Colt who designed the Sunningdale course. It was extended and improved later by the club's first professional, Tom Jones, who served the club for fifty-two years. Tourists find the course a demanding experience, and its quality was recognised when it became the venue for several top professional tournaments in the 1950s and 60s. Winners at this time were such golf wizards as Peter Allis, Henry Cotton, Harry Weetman, Peter Butler and Harry Bradshaw. The course is beautifully situated on the west-facing slopes of the peninsula, where the sea and mountain views add to its challenging golfing attractions.

A cockstride and a railway line separate the North Wales Course (shown here) from the Maesdu Course. In the 1950s when Henry Cotton played the course he called it 'a gem'. This is golfing riches indeed; a beautiful parkland course right next door to a traditional championship links. In its early years the course was affiliated to the Royal Liverpool Golf Club whose members had a significant influence on the development of golf throughout North Wales. The club was founded by Mr Tancred Disraeli Cummins assisted by Harold Hilton, the winner of two Opens in the 1890s. The club's first professional was Fred Collins (1894–1938) and he was succeeded by his nephew Sid (1938–79). The course has been the venue for many championship competitions including the Welsh Amateur in 1995. One of the holes named 'Hades' is recognised as being one of golf's finest short holes. The 17th is known as the LO hole, named after an unlikely event when two golfers, on first seeing it, said 'Ello, what do we 'ave 'ere?' Fierce winds from the sea, and wonderfully distracting views, make this a course to remember.

Formerly situated in Deganwy on Llandudno's West Shore, the Lido is, according to many people in the town, precisely what Llandudno is lacking at the moment. With regard to provision for family holidays the town seems to have lost its way, with, some would say, dire consequences for its future as a resort. The original Lido was built and opened in 1934. In addition to a large swimming pool of filtered sea-water there was a special pool for diving, with water chutes for the children. There was a restaurant with dancing and concert facilities, and even a small zoo. Eight thousand spectators could watch 1,000 swimmers, and ogle scantily clad bathing beauties in various contests. It was a complete centre for the holiday crowds, until, in the late 1950s, the inevitable happened: holiday crowds dwindled and a property developer stepped in. The valuable site was cleared and became a housing estate.

4

Llandudno & the Sea

Llandudno's long association with the sea is self-evident. Before the town was even thought of, the inhabitants of the village on Orme's Head relied on the sea for food, fuel, a livelihood and contacts with the outside world. Before the seaports and harbours were built, flat-bottomed boats appeared regularly with passengers and provisions. There are four on the very early panoramic photograph of the town shown above. All along the North Wales seaboard where there was a flatlanding on a beach and the right tidal conditions, they landed and traded. Sometimes in inclement weather the landing was at speed with an abrupt and unexpected ending, as the photographs on the following pages testify.

Two tragic photographs from the end of the nineteenth century: above, the wreck is on the West Shore and a pencil scribble on the reverse of the original photograph refers to it as being a Spanish ship. Note that the Bishop's Palace is a little further inland than it is now. Below, the wreck is on the North Shore, *c.* 1880, and is a particularly violent one. It is said that after a wreck, the inhabitants of the town were not averse to helping themselves to things that were not nailed down.

The *Flying Foam* of Bridgwater was the last wreck on the West Shore. Her cargo of coal is being unloaded here. She came to grief on 21 June 1936 after anchoring to repair a sail off Penmaenmawr. The violent storm dragged her on to the shore. When the tide is out and conditions are right the remains of her keel can still be seen, below.

LIFEBOATS

There has been a lifeboat at Llandudno for 140 years, the boat has been launched approximately 1,000 times and saved the lives of over 500 people. Nationally, the lifeboat service was founded in 1824, and it was thirty-seven years after the birth of the service in 1861 that the first boat arrived in Llandudno. The lifeboat station was built near the site of the existing railway station. The Irish sea is notoriously subject to westerly and south-westerly gales, and, when these blow, the North Wales coast presents a dreadful and inhospitable lee shore to sailing ships as there is no harbour or refuge of any great size. During such storms many boats sought refuge in Llandudno Bay, sometimes with dire consequences. The dominance of the Ormes' heads presents an obvious hazard in stormy weather, and in periods of limited visibility. The Great Orme has been well known to mariners of all nations throughout all time and has been called the Welsh 'Cape Horn'. In his excellent book, *Shipwrecks of North Wales* (1973 – revised and reprinted 2001) Ivor Wynne Jones maps the area around the Orme and Conway Bay and shows the astonishing number of shipwrecks over the years. A rapid increase in coastal traffic to the ports of Liverpool and Chester made the need for a lifeboat service all too apparent to the local population and the initiative of Revd M. Morgan and Mr John Jones prompted a visiting inspector to approve the application for a boat.

Left: The lifeboat bell used to be situated on the Promenade, before the maroon signals that are used to this day. This was part of the inadequate lifesaving apparatus provided by the Liverpool Docks Committee in 1815. The absence of a pier, and the Baths Hotel in its first phase of construction, suggests that this rare and unusual photograph was taken early in the town's history.

The first lifeboat house cost £147 10s, and the boat, a self-righter built by Forrest of Limehouse, cost £190. She was delivered free of charge by the London and North Western Railway on 15 January 1861. Watched by a large and enthusiastic crowd, Lady Augusta Mostyn smashed a bottle of wine over her bows and named her *The Sisters Memorial*. The boat was aptly named since the Misses Brown of Toxteth, Liverpool had donated the boat in memory of their dead sister. The first emergency callout was on 9 February 1861 but the Rhyl boat affected a rescue before the Llandudno boat arrived on the scene. In 1867 *The Sisters Memorial* was replaced by *The Sisters Memorial II* pictured here in 1887, her last year of service. *Sunlight No.1*, provided by the soap manufacturers Lever Brothers of Port Sunlight, replaced her.

Crew of the *Theodore Price*, *c.* 1915. The *Theodore Price* arrived on station in 1902. The boat had been chosen by the coxswain and two of the crew after they were sent by the RNLBI to visit other stations at various locations to pick the boat they considered most suitable for local conditions, an unusual management principle nowadays. She was a self-righting boat, 37ft long and powered by twelve oars. There were never any complaints about the performance of this boat during almost thirty years of service. The new boathouse was built more centrally to accommodate her, at a cost of £1,300.

The *Theodore Price* returns to shore.

From 1933 to 1953 the lifeboat was *The Thomas and Annie Wade Richardson* and this poignant photograph shows the people of the town awaiting her return from the most tragic call ever received by the Llandudno, or any other, station. The date is 2 June 1939, and the previous day is recalled with sadness in maritime history. *Thetis*, a new submarine commissioned in 1936, was undergoing trials in Liverpool Bay with 103 men on board. While she was some 14 miles off Llandudno she dived and failed to surface. Water had entered one of her torpedo tubes, flooding the forward compartments. The next day four men escaped using the Davis apparatus. The Llandudno boat was launched on 2 June to take Dr A. Madock Jones to HMS *Somali*, the naval vessel in attendance. The boat stood by and was eventually dismissed, and returned to Llandudno at 10.30 pm just after this photograph was taken. Dr Madock Jones commented later, 'unfortunately, my services were not needed'. The full horror of the occasion was difficult to accept, and the people in the silent crowd shown here would not forget their vigil. An elementary error in the shipyard had resulted in the deaths of 99 men in controversial and horrible circumstances. The Llandudno boat returned to the scene of the tragedy soon afterwards to lay a wreath. *Thetis* was connected to a salvage ship but the wire parted. She sank beneath the waves and was not seen again for five months, when she was raised and towed to Anglesey. *Thetis* was refitted and played a significant combat role as HMS *Thunderbolt*. She was sunk again by enemy action off Sicily in 1943.

In May 1963 a revolution occurred in the lifeboat service: a new type of boat was brought into use down the coast at Aberystwyth. This was the lightweight inshore dinghy (ILBs or 'D' Class lifeboats). Under 16ft long, it was built of neoprene-proofed nylon. It had a 40 hp outboard engine, achieved speeds of up to 20 knots with a crew of two or three, and could be launched at a fast rate. These boats were ideal for inshore use in places such as Llandudno where water sports are a feature of the summer scene. The first, No. 54, arrived at Llandudno in 1965 and was soon called out on 23 May to rescue a youth trapped on rocks. In October 1966, ILB 109 arrived at Llandudno; she cost £1,000 and was presented to the service appropriately by two local sisters. Between 1965 and 1991 the inshore boats were called out 516 times and saved 201 lives.

There is a great deal of valuable co-operation between the North Wales Lifeboat Service and RAF Valley, Anglesey.

On 30 January 1964 a new lifeboat arrived on station at Llandudno, built by Messrs Groves and Gutteridge of Cowes. This boat was heavier than previous ones and a new Case 1000 launching tractor T-73 arrived at the same time. She was self-righting, 37 feet long and equipped with two 52 hp diesel engines making 8 knots. The new boat was first called out in March of 1964 to a sailing incident. On 15 May the naming ceremony was carried out. After a service conducted by the Bishop of Bangor, Rt Revd G. Williams, the boat was christened *The Lilly Wainwright* by HRH Princess Marina, Duchess of Kent who was President of the RNLI. *The Lilly Wainwright* worked the Llandudno station for twenty-six years and left the service in 1990. She was regarded with deep affection by the people of the town and will never be forgotten by the fifty-eight people whose lives she saved in her 116 launches, averaging three or four successful missions annually.

The Lilly Wainwright, c. 1968.

In 1990 a new offshore boat arrived named the *Andy Pearce*, provided as a result of a legacy from Mr Andrew Pearce. This 12-metre Mersey class self-righter was built at the Cowes yard of FBM Ltd. The boat is powered by two 280 hp Caterpillar 3208-T diesel engines giving a top speed of 17 knots, double the speed of her predecessor. She cost £455,000 to build, an increase of £454,810 on the first boat to arrive on station 129 years earlier. There is controversy presently about the situation of the lifeboat house and its distance from its launching point on the Promenade. The RNLI would like to build a new station near the pier, but groups associated with the preservation of Llandudno's heritage oppose the plan, though they are not disputing the need for the boat to be nearer its launch point.

Lifeboat station, Lloyd Street.

PLEASURE STEAMERS

S. S. St. Elvies.

S. S. Snowdon.

Early visitors to the developing coastal towns arrived by boat and were transferred from ship to shore in small rowing boats. The building of piers and docks during the nineteenth century made life much easier. From the end of the nineteenth century until mid-way into the twentieth century pleasure steamers provided a nostalgic folk memory for the people of Merseyside and the Lancashire coast who began, increasingly, to visit North Wales. The steam packet *Cambria* was plying its trade between Liverpool and North Wales as early as 1821 (inaugural trip 4 June 1821). The original journeys were to Bagillt on the Dee Estuary; this was a disembarking point for Holywell which was a popular place for pilgrimages to St Winifrede's Well. In 1822 the packet-and-passenger service was extended in the newly built *Albion* to the Menai Strait, particularly Beaumaris, a developing holiday centre. There was soon fierce competition for this lucrative business. Prices for the service were very high, a single ticket probably costing the equivalent of a week's wages for an ordinary working man. The ships involved were small wooden paddle steamers ranging from 150 to 200 tons with 60–70 HP engines. Inevitably the urge for increased profits led to a skimping of service and safety, leading ultimately to the dreadful tragedy of the *Rothesay Castle* in 1831. A very old ship set out in bad weather, and as the journey proceeded the skipper became more and more drunk and incapable. His obdurate stupidity led ultimately to the death by drowning of 109 people on the Dutchman's Bank in the Menai Strait. From the plethora of companies vying for the trade the Liverpool and North Wales Steamship Company emerged triumphant, and it dominated from about 1882 until services ceased in the late 1950s.

A small family business competitor to the North Wales Steamship Company, the Snowdon Passenger Steamship Company had the *Snowdon* paddlesteamer (seen here *c*. 1910) as their main craft, built in 1892 by Laird Bros of Birkenhead. Eventually there was a merger and the *Snowdon* became part of the main fleet. She could accommodate about 450 passengers and transport them comfortably at a speed of 14 knots. From 1905 to 1907 she carried an average of 131 passengers on each of her trips from Llandudno to the Menai Strait calling at Caernarfon. She lasted for forty-one years and was disposed of in 1931.

The first *St Trillo*, *c*. 1915. There was another small and short-lived steamship company which traded under the name of the Colwyn Bay and Liverpool Steamship Company. In 1909 one of their paddlesteamers named the *Rhos Trevor* (built in 1876 and named 'Carisbrooke') was bought and was renamed the *St Trillo*. She had a passenger capacity of 463 and was used as a relief ship on high-days and holidays. She stayed with the company until 1921. Her sister ship the *Rhos Colwyn* sank off Rhos-on-Sea on 20 July 1908.

2,077 passengers could be carried swiftly and in luxurious conditions from Liverpool to Menai Strait. The passengers carried into Llandudno by this one ship added an enormous amount to the economic development of the town in the early years of the twentieth century. In her first year she carried 33,459 passengers to the town, averaging 500 per trip. This average increased to 605 per sailing during subsequent years. On one day in 1907 she brought in 1,830 excursionists She completed her farewell voyage on 28 September 1925; bedecked with bunting, she sailed to Menai Bridge, where she was greeted by schoolchildren who had been given a special holiday for the occasion. When she left Llandudno for the last time thousands of people saw her off singing 'Farewell my own true love' and there wasn't a dry eye in the house. She went to Briton Ferry where she was broken up. During her years of service she was estimated to have carried approximately four million happy passengers, and several thousand other-than-happy ones as a troopship in the First World War.

In 1904 'the finest vessel of her type afloat' arrived on the North Wales scene, and she was resplendent. *La Marguerite* was built in 1894 by the Fairfield Company for work on the Thames offering cross-channel services to Boulogne and Ostende calling at Margate. She did not last long there as the service proved to be unprofitable, she was offered for sale, and the Liverpool and North Wales Company snapped her up. She was the largest and best-equipped passenger paddle-steamer of her time, and her arrival at Liverpool caused a great deal of excitement. Her gross tonnage was 1,554 and she was 341ft in length.

Right: *La Marguerite* on her last passenger sailing, 1925.

La Marguerite at Llandudno Pier, *c.* 1912.

The early, Edwardian years of the twentieth century were the golden days and, during each summer, approximately 300,000 passengers were carried. Llandudno was the favoured port of call and, in 1907, a record number of people arrived at the pier aboard the company's ships *St Tudno*, *St Elvies* and *La Marguerite*, when a total of 3,181 people disembarked.

On board the *St Elian*, *c.* 1922.

The Liverpool & North Wales Steamship Co., Ltd.,

40 CHAPEL STREET, LIVERPOOL

WORKS' OUTINGS, CHOIR PARTIES, PICNICS, &c., to

LLANDUDNO & MENAI STRAITS

Via Liverpool and Steamer

SEASON 1929

BY THE TWIN-SCREW GEARED TURBINE SALOON STEAMER

"ST. TUDNO"

EASTER SAILINGS. 29TH MARCH TO 1ST APRIL AND DAILY.

COMMENCING SATURDAY, 18TH MAY, the Turbine Steamer "ST. TUDNO" (or "ST. ELVIES") leaves LIVERPOOL daily (Sundays included) at 10-45 a.m. for LLANDUDNO (allowing 4 hours ashore) and MENAI BRIDGE, due back about 7-30 p.m.

Reduced Fares are offered for the conveyance of Large and Small Parties, including Workpeople's Excursions, Choir Outings, Pleasure Parties, Picnics, &c.

SPECIAL PARTIES.—Parties of 10 or more can be booked at the following reduced fare for the day trip (Sundays 2/- extra) :—

LIVERPOOL and LLANDUDNO ..	7/- Saloon Return ..	5/- 2nd Saloon Return
LIVERPOOL and MENAI BRIDGE ..	9/- ,, ,, ..	7/- ,, ,,
ROUND ANGLESEY	11/- ,, ,, ..	9/- ,, ,,

First-Class Catering on board the Company's Steamers, Dinners at 4/- and Teas at 3/-, in First Class Dining Saloon. Menus can be submitted for Breakfast or Special Catering.

CHARTERS.—Subject to date being satisfactory, the vessels of the Company can be chartered for day return trips, Liverpool and Llandudno or Menai Straits, at low rates :—

**S.S. "ST. TUDNO" 2,493 Passengers. P.S. "ST. ELVIES" 991 Passengers.
P.S. "SNOWDON" 462 Passengers.**

TRANSFERABLE CONTRACTS.—Special transferable Season Contract Tickets are issued enabling Business Firms, Guilds and Clubs to purchase at low rates for individual use. Excursion Bookings to Liverpool for Boat Contractors.

Trip Secretaries and others desirous of making arrangements for same are requested to communicate with the LOCAL AGENTS, or

THE LIVERPOOL & NORTH WALES STEAMSHIP CO., Ltd.,

Telephone: 1654 CENTRAL **40 CHAPEL STREET, LIVERPOOL** *Telegrams* "ST. TUDNO," LIVERPOOL.

AGENTS :

MESSRS. THOS. COOK & SON LTD.,
31 FARGATE, SHEFFIELD

In 1926 the ship most people 'of a certain age' will remember, the *St Tudno*, arrived in North Wales. Her maiden voyage took place on Saturday 2 May 1926. She left Liverpool at 10.45 in the morning, and arrived back at 7.40 in the evening, carrying hundreds of passengers on that memorable day. She was one of the largest pleasure steamers afloat with an overall length of 329 feet, gross tonnage 2,326, and a speed of 19 knots. She was certified to carry 2,493 passengers. Luxury travel was epitomised by dining rooms, cafeterias, lounge bars and even a barber's shop. She was a screw ship, and unfortunately experienced difficulties with water depth in the Strait, so had to stop calling at both Beaumaris and Bangor. Her success led to the company deciding to replace all coal burning paddlers with more efficient turbine steamers. The *St Tudno* is seen here at Menai Bridge in about 1938.

During her time on the coast the *St Tudno* was accompanied by two smaller boats; the *St Seiriol II* (above) and the *St Silio* (later renamed *St Trillo*). The three steamers, in total, carried over a quarter of a million holiday excursionists a year. During the Second World War the ships were commandeered by the Admiralty for troop carrying and minesweeping duties. The *St Seiriol* played a big part in the evacuation of Dunkirk, making seven hazardous and action-packed voyages through the bombs and gun-fire.

St Trillo arrives at Amlwch on her maiden voyage. After the Second World War the company continued with a great deal of popularity for many years, but a combination of financial difficulties and several seasons of bad weather presented insurmountable problems. There was also the rise of cheap motoring with, by now, an almost universal car-owning population. The *St Seiriol* was sold in March 1962 to keep the wolf from the door, but it was not sufficient, and in 1962 the company went into voluntary liquidation and the *St Tudno* was sold for breaking. The *St Trillo* fought a rearguard action and continued a limited service from Llandudno until 1969, chartered to P&A Campbell of Bristol from Townsend Ferries. One hundred and fifty years of maritime history came to an end in 1969.

St Trillo off Great Orme's Head, *c*. 1956.

Two steamers still visit the pier annually, and enthusiasts eagerly await their arrival for a short stay. The *Balmoral* is a diesel motor vessel with a net tonnage of 310 and gross 736. She was built in 1949 and initially served as an Isle of Wight ferry, carrying passengers and cars from Southampton to Cowes. After a varied history she was transferred to Balmoral Excursions in the late 1980s. She joined the Waverley Steam Navigation Co. Ltd and subsequently she and the *Waverley* have gone from strength to strength.

Waverley is the last seagoing paddle steamer in the world. She was launched in 1946 replacing her namesake who was lost at Dunkirk in 1940. Her gross tonnage when built was 693, and she is powered by triple-expansion steam engines. By 1973 she was the only survivor of a considerable Scottish loch cruising fleet and was laid up for disposal. The Paddle Steamer Preservation Society snapped her up for the princely sum of £1, and they preserve her as closely as possible to her original condition. The Society and the Heritage Lottery fund have extensively overhauled and reboilered her. She now visits piers and ports all over the British Isles in an imaginative annual sailing programme, during which she gives delight to thousands of people.

5
Streets & People

Church Walks, *c.* 1920. This was one of the first roads built from the old village to connect it to the new church of St George's, which had been built in 1840 as a more convenient place of worship than St Tudno's. It was once the industrial heart of Llandudno with all the banging, clattering and dirt associated with copper mining. Water from the mine drove a large wheel which operated an ore crushing machine where Min-y-Don now stands. There were two Cornish steam engines further up the road at Ty Gwyn and behind the Empire Hotel. Before reaching the Empire Hotel above Ty Gwyn Road a glasshouse covers the opening to Kendrick's Cave, the significance of which is discussed in the earlier Great Orme chapter.

A rare photograph of an old part of the town. It is the entrance to Ty Gwyn Road, *c.* 1870, and shows many interesting features. At the halfway point up the Orme's cliff face is the wooden balcony which covers the entrance to Kendrick's home and cave (see page 16). Below the balcony is Rock Villa and below this are two miners' cottages. There had been a mineshaft just in front of the cottages so the miners did not have far to go to their work. It is said that in the filled-in shaft they planted an oak tree to commemorate the marriage (or coming of age) of Edward VII. The building on the left is now the Empire Hotel. When the photograph was taken it was Mander's Music Rooms with pianofortes for hire. A painted notice on the side of the building reminds the town that Thomas Williams has moved from the premises and has gone to Mostyn Street opposite the post office on what is now Hooson's Corner.

Ty Gwyn Road, 2001.

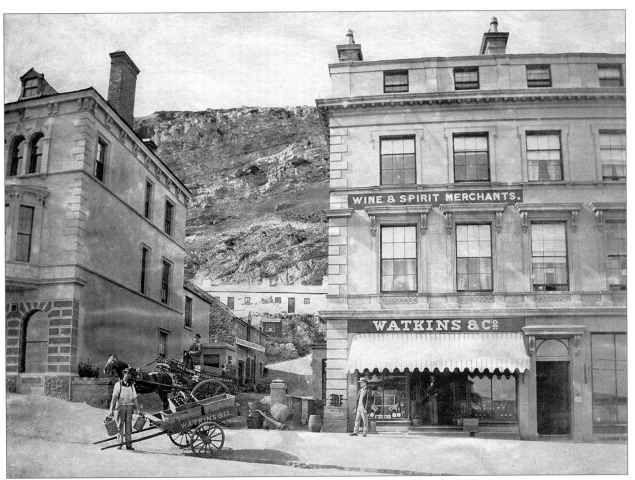

Tan-y-Ogof, *c.* 1878. On the right is the Empire Hotel and then a cul-de-sac, Tan-y-Ogof, which brings us to Bella Vista, which became the town's first bank, the National Provincial, in 1866. This block was the administrative hub of the developing town in the middle of the nineteenth century. Watkins & Co., wine and spirit merchants, occupy the end of what is now the Empire Hotel. Written on the photograph is the information that the wine store on the left-hand side of the cul-de-sac was the premises of the first printing works of the *Llandudno Advertiser*, the town's first newspaper.

Tan-y-Ogof, 2001.

The Empire Hotel area, *c.* 1870. Llandudno's first shopping mall was built in 1854 and housed a chemists, an Italian warehouse, and a grocer. The owner was Thomas Williams, who published a visitors' handbook, *Llandudno Its History and Natural History* in 1855, which, though a plagiarised version of an earlier work by Owen Williams, has proved to be an invaluable source of information for local historians ever since. The book also contains fifteen pages of closely printed lists of the merchandise he offered for sale; a cornucopia of oddities ranging from a 'Concentrated Compound Decoction of Sarsaparilla and Fluid Extract of Taraxacum' to 'Covered Pots for the Toilet'. These fifteen pages alone would provide the basis for a doctoral thesis on mid-nineteenth-century consumerism.

The Empire Hotel area today.

The Royal Hotel, *c.* 1880. Owen Williams noted the need for a hotel in the embryonic town in the auction brochure of 1849, which broke up the area into saleable lots. He indicated that a prospective hotel builder would be favourably considered in the auction. His town map contained plans for a medium-sized hotel to be known as the Mostyn Arms. This, the town's first important hotel, formed the basis for the extended Royal Hotel in Church Walks. The name change occurred because there was already a Mostyn Arms Hotel in the nearby village of Llanrhos. Goodness knows what possessed the town planners when they approved of the startlingly inappropriate building below.

Mostyn Street begins and runs at right angles to Church Walks with the impressive Empire Hotel at its head. On the right of this photograph, at Court Street, there was the town's centre of law and order between 1854 and 1915. The first constable earned the princely sum of 16s a week in 1854. The town first hosted a National Eisteddfod in a field off Upper Mostyn Street near the Baptist chapel in 1864, with seating for 6,000 visitors. Extreme poverty once pervaded the town as a result of seasonal unemployment and very low pay for hotel workers. Prosperous hoteliers were being enriched by exploitation. An attempt to alleviate starvation was made behind the Masonic Hall at No. 108, on the left of the picture below, with the establishment of a soup kitchen where meals of soup and bread cost 1d. The picture of prosperous Llandudno as an area of deprivation and poverty is difficult to grasp, but winter conditions were appalling and even today, with pathetic minimum wage levels, employment prospects are not good once the summer season is over.

Upper Mostyn Street, 2001.

Edward Owen's butcher's shop, *c.* 1890. Edward Owen was the town's first butcher. It is said that he set up his first business from the same shed on the foreshore in which the town was planned. This carnage is a sight of limited appeal to modern eyes though commonplace before the war. The amount of meat consumed is a sensitive indicator of the wealth of a society. Prior to the importation of refrigerated meat at relatively low prices, meat eating was, to a large extent, a middle- and upper-class prerogative. The author recalls that, even in the 1930s, meat was an occasional rather than a regular adornment of the working-class table, more often than not some kind of cheap offal. Butchers' shops varied in quality from the high class 'purveyors' of fresh-killed produce, to those at the lowest end ('slink' butchers) who sold meat of dubious origin from animals that had died in mysterious circumstances. Generally speaking, the higher end of the trade was represented by permanent premises, apprentices, and a delivery service. The shop shown here fulfils all of those criteria. Nowadays, the independent butcher is becoming a part of folk memory as more people buy their meat pre-packed, pre-cooked and pre-digested from the supermarket shelves.

The shopfront today, with preserved sign.

It is difficult to conceive of Edwardian Llandudno as a hotbed of insurrection and revolutionary politics, but so it was in the early years of the twentieth century (1907). This modest backstreet café, The Cocoa House, became a centre for the suffragette cause in North Wales. In stormy meetings in front of the Marine Hotel, interrupted by raucous music hall songs and ill-mannered hectoring by drunken men, ladies such as Miss Mary Gawthorpe addressed the crowds, espousing the cause of Votes for Women. The council, as is their wont, stepped in and banned them from speaking, but the local press supported them and praised their eloquence. In 1914 there was an unsuccessful attempt by the agitators to set fire to the pier in the furtherance of their cause. The Cocoa House has another and very important claim to fame. It was the centre of Llandudno's fight against the demon drink. At the end of the nineteenth century drunkenness was a national problem in Great Britain, and it was estimated that at any one time at least 25 per cent of the population of London and other cities would be drunk. Gin in those days was almost as cheap as water. The Cocoa House opened in 1883 to provide a meeting place as an alternative to the prevailing tavern culture. The building became a centre for the Temperance Movement. It dispensed food and non-alcoholic beverages, namely coffee and cocoa, to the ordinary people of the town. The extent of poverty locally was mentioned earlier, and the Cocoa House fought this also, acting as a charitable institution which provided penny dinners. Nowadays the teetotalism has gone and it is permitted to drink wine with a meal.

Opposite: Indoor market stalls, *c.* 1900, and their site today. Behind Mostyn Street and near the Cocoa House there used to be a closed market of significant ugliness and redolent smells. This was built by the local council in 1897 and pulled down almost a hundred years later in somewhat controversial circumstances. It is now a car park, which, it is believed, will itself soon be closed so that another shopping facility will come to the town. More traffic chaos is bound to follow.

Mostyn Street, Bunney's Corner, *c.* 1878.

In the early years, Mostyn Street's buildings provided accommodation for the increasing numbers of Victorian tourists, and could be described as 'bed and breakfast' boarding houses. Early photographs show a dusty, unsurfaced street and unpaved house frontages. It was only later that pavements, verandas, and shop windows appeared. From these Victorian origins, shown here in the 1870s and 1880s, the street has become North Wales's premier shopping street.

This is the corner of Mostyn Street and Lloyd Street and we can see R. Roberts and Son, the Royal Fish Stores. The shop was founded very early in the town's history in 1854. Next door is John Jones, the self-proclaimed 'Purveyors By Special Royal Warrant' of meat; he was calling himself the Queen's Butcher in 1882. The Royal Fish Stores in retaliation called themselves 'Purveyors of fish to the Royal Court of Roumania', following the visit of the Queen of Roumania in 1890. This photograph was taken before then and the decorations on John Jones' shop contains a message in Welsh which congratulates the Old Queen on her Golden Jubilee, which dates the photograph at about 18 June 1887. The Royal Fish Stores eventually moved into Lloyd Street, and the photograph below was taken there showing off a true fishermans' tale, a sturgeon caught in the river at Conway. Top left, is the same scene today.

This rare photograph of central Mostyn Street *c.* 1880 shows much that has changed over the years. The single storey building just beyond the shop is Llandudno's first library built in 1873. The present library was built on the same site in 1910 and was opened by Lord Mostyn on 15 September of that year. Next to the library is Zion Baptist Chapel, which was built in 1862. Mostyn Estates controversially pulled this down in 1967 after they had refused to renew its lease, and, I suggest, that this had something to do with the commercial value of the site?

The same view today.

Site of Baptist chapel, 1980.
Though the Zion chapel was not the
most beautiful of buildings, what
replaced it was worse. This
undistinguished row of concrete
boxes squatted on the side of the
street for twenty-five years until the
new Victoria Centre replaced it. The
tree on the right of the picture was
planted to commemorate the first
wedding held in Zion in 1877.
When the Victoria Centre was being
built the developers wanted to
remove the tree but had to give in to
local demand to leave it where it
was. They were forced to build a
special depression in the canopy to
accommodate the branches. The
tree had the last laugh when it
succumbed to Dutch Elm disease
shortly after the opening.

Victoria Centre, 2001.

Across the road from Victoria Centre is the national institution, Marks and Spencer's. It arrived in the town in 1936 and over the years has added considerably to the town's commercial life. The store attracts shoppers from all over North Wales with the usual advantages that this brings to other commercial enterprises. The shop was enlarged in 1972, and a second building completed in the 1990s. The site was originally occupied by the manse of the English Wesleyan church which had stood there since 1866. The garden of the manse can be seen on the right of the photograph. Over the years there has been criticism of the building style which does not conform to the regulations laid down by the Improvement Commissioners, and this was noted when the second building was erected.

M&S today.

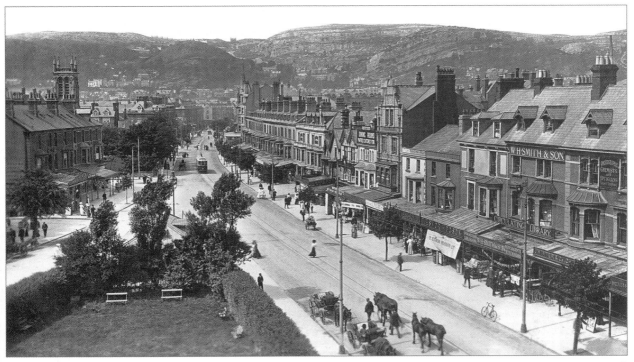

The photographs on this page show the beginnings of a change which was to have far-reaching effects. The period during which these two photographs were taken was one of spacious and leisurely thoroughfares for pedestrians. Hidden in the photograph below, taken at about the end of the First World War, are some of the first motor cars, ready to pounce and take over. The years between the two World Wars witnessed the first stirrings of today's unpleasant, car-jammed streets. Prior to this, the middle-class aspiration was to have a live-in domestic servant as a status symbol. Both of the author's grandmothers were 'in service', but, by 1931, only 5 per cent of households still had servants, and the aspiration had changed to motor car ownership. In 1921 there were 200,000 private cars in Britain but within eighteen years this number had risen to two million. There are today some 26 million, with two and a half million new cars sold every year. In the past year or so Llandudno has introduced traffic calming techniques and made spaces for people where once there were cars. This is a welcome and positive approach to town centre traffic problems, but it has not met with the approval of many shop owners. Predictably, there will be a great deal of opposition to any further attempts at pedestrianisation.

Postwar Mostyn Street, *c.* 1949 (above) and in 2001 (below). If the Improvement Commissioners were to return to the town today they would be horrified at what time has done to their wide, airy boulevards. Now they are clogged with stinking traffic and hapless pedestrians risking their lives on the assault course between pavements. Both sides of the road are packed with parked vehicles narrowing the traffic stream dangerously. Radical measures are called for, which, it has been suggested, include improved car parking facilities on the edge of town and wholesale pedestrianisation of the town centre. But there are other issues: the Improvement Commissioners established building standards that were elegant, eye-catching and practical. These are now being ignored, and we see in Llandudno the worrying trend that is becoming the norm in Britain's high streets: the monolithic domination of a few powerful shop chains that is leading to a boring lack of diversity in architectural and planning terms. The price of 'progress' is the loss of quality and uniqueness. The high cost of town-centre property and business rates are driving out the smaller independent shopkeeper, and these are being replaced by banks, building societies and insurance companies. As a result, Mostyn Street is gradually losing its distinctive character.

Gloddaeth Street and Avenue, *c.* 1910 (above) and Gloddaeth Avenue, *c.* 1912 (below). Stretching across the Creuddyn from shore to shore, a distance of 1,380 yards, Gloddaeth Street starts in Prince Edward Square, recently redesigned to make it more pedestrian-friendly and pleasing to the eye. The square was chosen as the site of the 1864 Gorsedd (bardic crowning ceremony) stone circle. A dominant feature of the town's landscape is the War Memorial, a structure of classical beauty commemorating two world wars. On this road between 1934 and 1989 Llandudno's most prominent building stood, the Astra Theatre and Winter Gardens and the Odeon cinema. The site, formerly a market garden known as The Vineyard, is now occupied by a block of retirement flats. From 1907 to 1956 Gloddaeth Street was the tram route from the town to the West Shore. The photograph below clearly shows the lack of development on the West Shore at this time, so the trams did not always complete the journey to the terminus. They went on to the West Shore only at the passengers' request, and frequently ended their journey at Hooson's Corner.

You have to look at the Orme's configuration to work out the location of this photograph. It was taken from Chapel Street looking up Arfon Avenue, with Gloddaeth Street crossing it centrally, *c.* 1880. Missing from the view are the Clarence Hotel and Seilo Welsh chapel, which have not yet been built. The wooden structure is a newspaper stand selling the *Llandudno Register and Herald* which claimed to publish a list of all the visitors to the town every Saturday morning, an idiosyncratic selling ploy. The photograph below shows the changes that have occurred over the years.

Madoc Street, *c*. 1910. Space precludes a detailed consideration of all of the streets surrounding the town centre but they all have their own story. Madoc Street, which runs parallel with central Mostyn Street, deserves consideration because of its link with the early town. When the town was being planned, the prime sites on the waterfront and in the Church Walks area were occupied by squatters in some twenty-five cottages. Lord Mostyn ruthlessly evicted these impediments to his financial advancement and housed the evictees in Madoc Street. They could have stayed in their homes, since they had a perfect right to do so according to the ancient Welsh custom, *ty un nos* (one-night house). By a typical piece of landlord skulduggery Mostyn forced a nominal rent from most of the squatters, and thus deprived them of their legal rights, leading to their subsequent removal.

A quiet Chapel Street (formerly North Madoc Street) in 1908 awaits the traffic chaos that is to come. Today this street has the distinction of being both 'topped and tailed' with a fish and chip shop and a place of worship.

In the years 1999 and 2000 the North Western Gardens area was given a long-needed facelift. This has not only improved the appearance of this part of the town but has also made it more pedestrian-friendly. Rerouting the traffic has reduced the dangers of fast-moving vehicles and created space for people to sit and relax. This project, along with a similar one at the other end of town in Prince Edward Square, provides a model for what needs to be done elsewhere.

The photographs above and left were taken on the same day in 1902; three horse-drawn steam pumps form a parade and a ladder rescue demonstration from the roof of St George's Hotel. The first fire brigade was formed in Llandudno in 1854, very early in the town's history. The five-man fire-fighting team had available only the most basic of equipment; a couple of ladders, some buckets and a hose. This was the situation for about twenty years until 1874 when a horse-drawn Merryweather hand pump was purchased and stored in Market Street. In 1882 a steam pump was installed and called the St Tudno. A petrol-driven fire engine came to the town in 1925. The new fire station below was built in 1970.

May Day celebrations were an important feature of the town's communal life. It was a colourful day of parades, carnivals and a celebration of youthful beauty in the crowning of the May Queen. The streets were decorated with bunting and the townspeople stretched their imaginations in the creation of carnival floats and bizarre costumes. Apart from its pagan significance, the 'feast of Beltain' was of particular importance to Llandudno because it heralded the start of the holiday season, a period of employment and financial security. Today there are few vestiges of the spirit that prevailed from about 1892 to the mid-1950s. The event is now called a Victorian Extravaganza and lasts a long May bank holiday weekend, with parades and vintage vehicle displays, when thousands of visitors flock to the town to be entertained in a heady atmosphere of fairground rides and street entertainments. The event may now be more commercial than previously but it is a thoroughly enjoyable weekend and helps to boost the town's flagging fortunes.

LAND TRANSPORT

A mark of social position was the possession of one's own horse-drawn transportation. The early photograph above taken in Church Walks shows a donkey cart under the control of a child clearly too young to drive it. The term 'carriage trade' originated at this time to indicate that those so called were either middle- or upper-class, certainly well off, since keeping a horse was a costly business. Below, a crowded four-in-hand is preparing for a trip from the North Western Hotel at the turn of the nineteenth century.

Camera Hill and Pavilion. The era of motor transport is just dawning. Horse-drawn cabs are a prominent feature in turn-of-the-century photographs of Llandudno's street life. They stood in ranks down the middle of Mostyn Street, near the railway station, or near the pier waiting for the steamer trade. In the photograph above they are in Prince Edward Square for journeys along the Promenade or around the Marine Drive. A large proportion of Llandudno's population was involved in this seasonal occupation which, considering the circumstances, did not provide an opulent living. In 1902 there were an estimated 3.5 million horses in Great Britain and this large number caused many social problems. True, a large labour force was devoted to horse care and the provision of carriages, stabling, grooming, coachmen,

smiths, etc. but annually each horse eats the product of 4 or 5 acres of land, somewhere between 5 and 6 tons of fodder. Horse droppings in town centres were unhygienic and led to the permanent employment of crossing sweepers. An estimated 10 million tons of droppings were deposited in Britain each year. We complain of the pollution left by the internal combustion engine; consider the situation if every car in the country were to be replaced by a horse-drawn carriage. . . .

Mostyn Street, early twentieth century.

Above, an excursion is about to start from the County Hotel in Craig-y-Don, *c.* 1910, and the one seen right is stopping at the Tal-y-Cafn (Ferry) Hotel in the Conway Valley for a refreshment break. These splendid vehicles, some 'four-in-hand', presented an imposing and picturesque spectacle. Llandudno's first horse-drawn omnibus ran from St George's Hotel to Conway station. Some early postcards show horse-drawn buses on the Promenade (see opposite). Their main function, however, seems to have been excursions into the countryside around Llandudno and up the Conway Valley into magical Snowdonia.

Buses line up outside the Clarence Hotel, Gloddaeth Street. The first motor omnibus in Great Britain ran in the streets of Edinburgh in 1898; their potential caught on, and they spread rapidly throughout Great Britain. They presented a less labour-intensive and less costly service than horse buses but, more importantly, they were a more humane method of transporting large numbers of people uphill. The railway companies ran many of these early motor omnibus services, using them as road links between stations and small rural communities.

Mostyn Street, 2001.

TRAMWAYS

Bodafon Fields and Little Orme, *c.* 1915. Travelling between Llandudno and its neighbours Rhos-on-Sea and Colwyn Bay at the end of the nineteenth century was a hazardous and wearisome journey, either on foot over unmade roads, or by rail via Llandudno Junction and the branch line through Deganwy to Llandudno. Some sort of public transport link became imperative for the mutual development of the towns, and this apparent need attracted the interest of electric tramway companies, several of which put forward abortive proposals in the 1890s. The Llandudno and Colwyn Bay Light Railway Order 1898 was accepted in 1899 by the Board of Trade, and the construction of the line was scheduled. Nothing happened for seven years of legal shilly-shallying and failed attempts to raise money. In 1904 the name of the company changed to Llandudno and Colwyn Bay Traction Co. Ltd. After repeated applications for time extensions to the Board of Trade, work began on the line, but with little discernible progress. In 1906 the company went into liquidation. There was another name change to Llandudno and District Electric Traction Construction Co. Ltd, and from this point work gathered pace. By the end of July 1907 the section between Rhos-on-Sea and West Parade, Llandudno was ready for inspection. In 1909 there was a final name change to the Llandudno & Colwyn Bay Electric Railway Limited.

Tram shelter, West Shore, 2001. This attractive circular building is a refurbishment by Llandudno Council of a tram shelter put here originally by the Llandudno and Colwyn Bay Electric Railway Company in 1907. It is one of the few tangible remnants of the old system. From this point, though there is little evidence of it now, the line turned sharp left and headed for Deganwy along West Parade to Dale Street. The section was little used and so the trams tended to terminate at this shelter, and the extension ceased to exist. In fact, the section from this terminus to the corner of Mostyn Street (Hooson's Corner) was very little used in the early days because the urbanisation of the West Shore area was lagging well behind the development of the town centre and North Shore. For this reason, trams tended to start and finish their journeys at Hooson's Corner for the first six months or so of the line's existence. Later still, it became clear that the system from Hooson's Corner to the West Shore was very little used, and it became 'at request' for the tram to complete the journey.

Hooson's Corner and Gloddaeth Street in the 1950s.

Inaugural run by tram No. 14, Mostyn Street, 1907. Sunday 19 October saw the first run of the service, a tram started at each end of the line at Rhos-on-Sea and Llandudno at 9 am on a cold and blustery day. J. Fred Francis and Sons linked the tram at Rhos-on-Sea with the town centre at Colwyn Bay (fare 3*d*).The trams were to run a half-hourly service from 9 am, and a 15-minute service from 12 noon to 10.30 pm, six days a week, but never on the sacrosanct Welsh Sunday. The immediate response of the public was enthusiastic, and crowds filled the trams all through the first day when 4,434 passenger journeys were made. Receipts were in excess of £45.

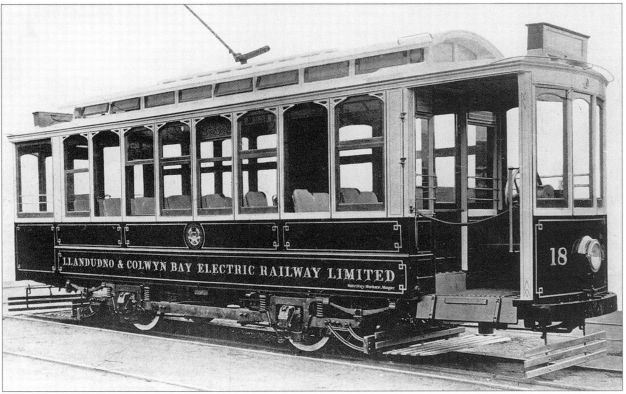

Tram Nos 15 to 18 were four-wheeled, semi-convertible cars which arrived in September 1909. The United Electric Car Co. Ltd built them in Preston. They could carry thirty-one passengers seated. They were dark red in colour, with cream and gold lining, the new name of the company proudly running the length of the car. The staff called them 'Yankees' because of their foreign appearance. This stock was renowned for the squealing noise it made on the tight curves on parts of the track, particularly at Hooson's Corner, and there was a great deal of complaint from residents. The cars were withdrawn in 1936 and stored until 1941. The bodies were eventually sold for sheds in the army camps of Rhyl and Bodelwyddan.

Space precludes a detailed discussion of the system's rolling stock but there are several books available containing this information. One type of car is mentioned here because of its tremendous popularity with the tourists in the area. This was the 'Toastrack', seen here in Colwyn Bay in the 1950s. This type of tram was first ordered in 1914, but the order was not completed until 1920 because of the intervention of the First World War. There was seating for sixty passengers on fourteen full-width, liftover bench seats, with two half-width, liftover seats on either side of the trolley mast. Their popularity with summer visitors was immediate, presumably because of their similarity to the Big Dipper rollercoaster. The ride down Little Orme cutting was particularly exhilarating, and many drivers ensured that the passengers received a thrill here. These trams continued in popularity until the demise of the line in 1955.

Coming down the Little Orme cutting, *c.* 1955. A country prospect presented itself to top-deck passengers as the tram left Mostyn Broadway, crossed Nant-y-Gamar road, and proceeded towards Craigside over the track cut through Bodafon Fields. There was the expectation of the climb up Penrhyn Hill and the rush down the Little Orme cutting into Penrhyn Bay.

Below: a rare photograph of a track-laying team at work in Bodafon Fields in the early days of the line's development.

The Budget tollgate, *c.* 1950.

A mixture of national politics and transport history is presented in this photograph. In 1908 Lloyd George introduced an Old Age Pensions Act which awarded the princely sum of 5*s* a week for the over-70s and 7*s* 6*d* a week for married couples. In anticipation of having to pay more taxes to fund this, a local landowner, William Horton, decided to erect a gate and levy a toll on anyone using the shore road. He sold the road eventually (1911) to the tram company, which continued to exact a toll until 1961 when the company was liquidated. The liquidators then collected the money until 1963, when Llandudno and Colwyn Bay Councils purchased the road. The toll collector for many years was Nat Chadderton, an ex-tramways employee, who was still taking the money at 87 years of age.

Flooded tramway and golf course, 1952. The proximity of the line to the sea at various points was obviously a potential hazard and there were several occasions when the sea broke through and did considerable damage at Llandudno's West Shore and at Penrhyn Bay. This photograph shows the effects of such a breach in the sea defences in Penrhyn Bay. In 1947, and again in 1952, ferocious gales raised gigantic waves which battered the North Wales coast; the waves undermined the tracks, making them dangerous. There were abortive attempts to protect the tracks by dragging up boulders from the beach and back-filling them, but it was clear that strong sea walls were required. The company was eventually forced to introduce single-track working at this point, which became permanent from 1952. The sea walls, under construction in the photograph below, and funded by central government, were eventually built in the late 1950s.

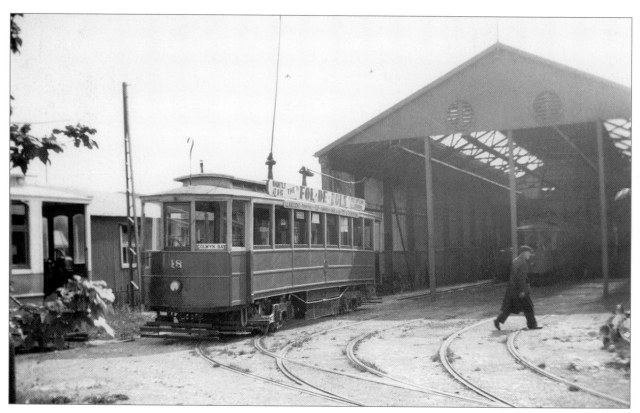

Old tramway depot, Penrhyn Bay, 1950s. The tram depot was built in Penrhyn Bay in 1907 and provided covered accommodation for some twenty trams in an eight-lane terminus. It was built so that it could provide all of the space and equipment necessary for the efficient running and servicing of the whole system. The site was on approximately 1¼ acres in an area known locally as The Klondike because it was in the 'back of beyond'. The site is still linked with transport, as a depot for a national freight company.

Colwyn Bay terminus, *c.* 1914. Local controversies about route choice delayed the completion of the system into Colwyn Bay. The company wanted to link the system directly with the railway station in the town but it never did. Work began apace compared with the rate of progress in the early years. The service to Colwyn Bay opened on 7 June 1908, and in 1912 the company sought permission to continue the line on into Old Colwyn where it would terminate at the Queen's Hotel near Penmaen Head. This section was completed and opened on 26 March 1915, the line being now 8.14 miles long.

In the early 1950s the company began to experience difficulties. There was a distinct lack of investment, particularly as the line was being subjected to fierce competition from the bus companies, electricity supply was also problematic and, above all, the popularity of the family car was making local transport increasingly unnecessary. The tramway was adding problems to roads becoming congested with traffic. The last tram completed the route on Saturday 24 March 1956, and on that day the trams were packed with people anxious to pay their last respects to a system which had been regarded with such affection. The photograph here showing the eventual destiny of one of the early trams tells its own story.

Great Orme Tramway, *c.* 1905. Roads, lanes and pathways have existed on the Great Orme from time immemorial, but with the expansion of housing, activities on the summit and increasing tourism it became clear that something was required for the easier transportation of people and goods up its steep gradients. At the end of the nineteenth century there were suggestions that a funicular (cable) railway might fill the bill. It was further suggested that a ride on the funicular would act as a tourist attraction. A consortium of local businessmen and well-to-do local residents made proposals for the tramway as we know it today, and in the winter of 1897/8 they promoted a Parliamentary bill for permission to build the line. It took two years for the legal and bureaucratic process to be cleared before the scheme was given the go-ahead in October 1900. In April 1901 contractors were appointed and construction began.

Tram station, 2001. Work began at the bottom in April 1901, and initially progress was slow. The steel cables were not delivered until May 1902 and at the end of that month, trial runs were in progress. On Wednesday 30 July 1902, Colonel Von Donop of the Board of Trade inspected the lower section and approved of it. Formal operations began on the next day as the tourist season was in full flow. By 8 October 1902 the line had carried 70,000 passengers.

The halfway station, 1950s. The second section to the summit was completed in 1903, and, because of the lack of steep gradient, proceeded more quickly. The complete service to the summit began on 8 July 1903. In the 1903 season a total of 77,410 passengers was carried.

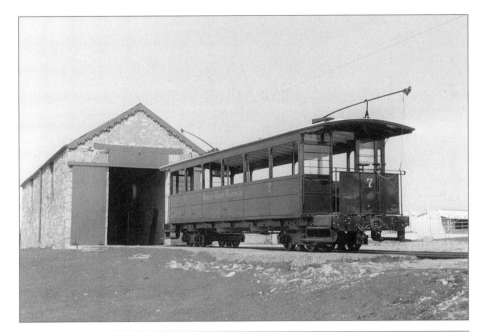

New halfway station, 2001. In May 2000 there was a collision between two of the trams, which resulted in slight injuries to twenty-one passengers, and the line was closed for modifications. It reopened in July 2001. A concerted effort is being made to boost the tramway as a tourist attraction with a cash injection of £40,000 over three years. The aim is to increase passenger figures by 30,000 per annum by the year 2006. The Heritage Lottery Fund is also providing money for maintenance and construction work until 2006 and a marketing officer is being appointed.

ENTERTAINMENT

Before the building of theatres the townspeople and visitors were entertained in the streets by itinerant players such as are shown here in very early photographs. Scrawled in faint pencil on the back of the young duo is the appellation 'Italian Bagpipe players'. The lad without the instrument appears to be dancing a jig. In the photograph below the hurdy-gurdy man is accompanied by his wife, who is controlling a little monkey on the end of a string. This photograph was taken in Church Walks and probably dates from the 1870s. In the early years the burgeoning town attracted large numbers of itinerant musicians and entertainers and the resulting cacophony caused a great deal of distress to the residents; at one time as many as eight or ten bands were playing in the town at the same time. Action was needed to curb the ensuing bedlam and the Commissioners rushed through by-laws to this effect in the 1870s.

Hurdy-gurdy man and wife, 1870s.

The theatres in the Happy Valley have an unfortunate history: several have been destroyed by fire, and nothing is there at the moment because of an act of vandalism some forty or so years ago. The first theatre was a canvas bell-tent used as a dressing and prop room by a husband and wife team of minstrels. Later structures were ornately decorated with oriental grandeur. The shows attracted large audiences, many of whom managed to evade the persistence of the 'bottler' who moved among them soliciting funds to defray expenses. The ornate theatre façade is in the background, and the 'bottler' is on Aberdeen Hill, blacked up as a minstrel in a white coat, in the foreground, in a scene dating from the 1920s.

In 2001, the 'theatre' has gone.

Churchill's Happy Valley Minstrels, late nineteenth century. This extremely rare studio portrait shows the troupe blacked up and striking poses. The names scrawled on the back of the cabinet photograph are Diddier, Perry, Aubun, Allan, Uncle, Molnne (?), Githerington, Miller, Gata, and on the extreme right Billy Churchill himself. Billy was a nationally famous entertainer who played in the very first Royal Command Performance at the Palace Theatre, London, in 1912. The Perry and Allan named are probably the ones who later formed their own concert party (see opposite). The Churchill troupe has doubled in number in the Happy Valley theatre photograph below.

Perry and Allan's Minstrels have strayed from their usual venue in the Happy Valley and have come to town to perform. Busking was probably an appetiser to whet the appetites of the tourists and entice them to the main show in the open-air theatre. Perry and Allan's Happy Valley Minstrels were a group of sixteen or so men (early photographs show no lady performers) who performed on the Orme in the 1890s. Boy Perry later called himself Laddie Cliff, achieving fame before the turn of the century as a London musical comedy star with the internationally renowned company, The Co-Optimists.

Perry and Allan's Happy Valley Minstrels, *c.* 1890.

There is no reference in the literature to the Orme's summit being a place of professional theatre, but this photograph of about 1912, with a tram in the background, shows a performing troupe of minstrels playing from a simple canvas tent. Another group of players calling themselves The Scarlet Merrions performed on the side of the Orme in a wooden shed near Faulke's Cave (see below). It would seem that in the early years of the nineteenth century it was difficult not to be entertained wherever you looked in Llandudno; sadly, not the case today.

Punch and Judy on the Promenade, *c.* 1912 (above) and today (below). Punch and Judy has a long history. The first printed record of the story appeared in a book published in 1828. It was written by John Payne Collier, illustrated by George Cruikshank and published by Edward Prowett. They had visited Giovanni Piccini, a renowned performer, and made detailed notes and sketches of his performances. Doubts have been expressed about the authenticity of the performance as a true representation of the story passed down through the ages, but it is considered to be a fairly accurate narrative. Piccini achieved a degree of immortality following its publication. He was said to have been a Punch and Judy man for some fifty years before the visit. Glove puppetry has a much longer history and the literature of the Tudors and Stuarts indicates that it was a well-liked form of entertainment. Samuel Pepys records his delight at a show given by 'Signor Bologna alias Pollicinella' in Covent Garden Square in 1662. Many Italian puppeteers followed Pollicinella to England, and the puppet, later corrupted to 'Punchinello', became a very popular figure. Pollicinella even performed before the King. The tradition lives on in Llandudno with its base at Punchinello Cottage.

Richard Codman, *c.* 1875. If Richard Codman arrived in Llandudno today and set up his Punch and Judy show he would be met with the same hostility from the authorities as he was when he set up his business in 1864. If the Improvement Commissioners had had their way this nationally loved figure, an inspiration to Charles Dickens and loved by millions of children through the years, would never have performed on the Promenade. As it was, his early shows were said to have taken place in the Church Walks area in the vicinity of the Empire Hotel. He fought the commissioners and won, and a tradition was born which lives to this day, almost 140 years later, with the business still in the hands of the Codman family.

The Codman family's collection of puppets.

Codman's 'horseless' caravan.

Richard Codman arrived in a caravan, and his horse, it is alleged, dropped dead, so he had to stay. This rare and historic photograph is believed by the family to be the very caravan in which he arrived. Legend has it that he carved his first puppets from driftwood gathered from the beach. He died in 1909 and his son Herbert took over the business and ran the show until he also died in 1961. One of Richard's other sons, John, went up a different showbusiness avenue, and played an important part in the development of the cinema, running an early fairground-style travelling bioscope. He also ran a minstrel group in the Happy Valley theatre (see below) and, in the winter, his travelling company of entertainers performed in traditional theatre venues.

May Day at Codman's Happy Valley theatre, *c.* 1920.

Richard's grandson, John (Jack) Codman, took over the business in 1961 after serving a twenty year apprenticeship with his father Herbert, and ran it for another twenty years until his death in 1980. Jack was the puppeteer my children loved, and his forty-year sojourn on the Promenade thrilled and delighted thousands and thousands of children. Now they in their turn are bringing their children and grandchildren to see the 'Comic Tragedy'. The two photographs on this page are of Jack Codman outside Punchinello Cottage in the 1970s.

The business, traditional as ever and still thriving, is now in the hands of Jack's daughter, Jacqueline Millband and her husband Morris, who run it with the aid of their son Jason. They were recently the subjects of a television programme depicting the arts in Wales, and a new issue of Punch and Judy commemorative postage stamps was launched on the Promenade in August 2001.

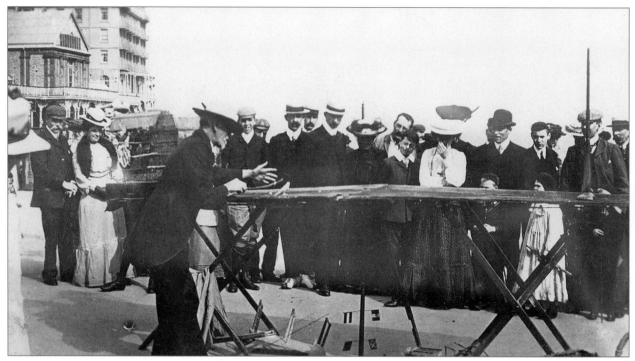

Another entertainer who would receive short shrift if he were to appear on the Promenade now was Sgr Giciano Ferrari with his performing birds. A man of obvious Italian descent, he came to Llandudno towards the end of the nineteenth century and stayed until his death in 1923. His entertaining performances on the pier and Promenade attracted large crowds of holidaymakers. This unusual view from behind Ferrari shows some of the interesting bits and pieces he used in the act: ladders and tightropes, a flagpole for 'flags of all nations', and a miniature carriage to be pulled by birds in harness.

Crowds 'flock' to Sgr Ferrari on the Promenade, 1920s.

The Arcadia Theatre, *c.* 1938. The photograph below will bring a tear to the eye and a lump to the throat of many people. This squalid, unkempt disintegrating building is what is left of the theatre in the picture above, which for over one hundred years gave so much unalloyed pleasure to thousands. Many great theatrical names trod the boards here since it opened as the Victoria Palace in July 1894. It was to have been part of an additional pier complex that was never realised. Jules Riviere had fallen out with the existing pier's management and formed a company to build a rival complex at this point, complete with pier jutting into the bay. In about 1907 the theatre was stripped of its 1,200 seats and it became a noisy and exciting rollerskating rink. The theatre underwent several name changes in its early life: Riviere's Concert Hall, Llandudno Opera House, the Hippodrome, and finally, under the direction of the famous impresario Will Catlin, it became the Arcadia. Like the Pier Pavilion before it, it is being left to rot, and most people would prefer to see it die with dignity, but, as usual, the powers that be do not seem to care.

A happy occasion in 1951 was the great impresario Will Catlin's eightieth birthday. He is standing right of centre, toasting the assembled party, many of whom were part of Catlin's unforgettable shows over the years.

The shape of things to come: the Pier Pavilion conflagration of 1994, when the town lost one of its major architectural assets.

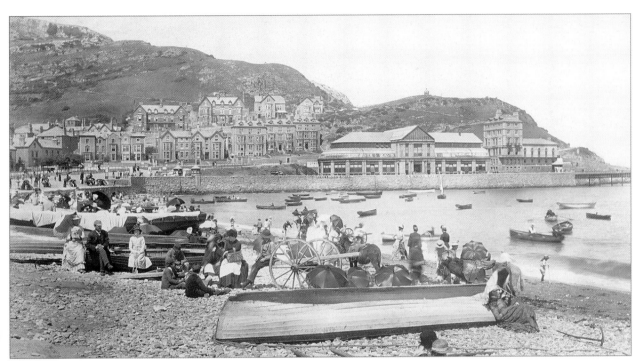

Pier Pavilion from the beach, *c.* 1890. The Pier Pavilion was a beautiful building and was at one time the main venue for shows and entertainment. The resident 'character' was Jules Riviere, a colourful conductor with a volatile personality. He conducted the orchestra facing the audience so that they could get a full view of his impressive technique. Originally he had conducted his small band in the bandstand seen earlier but, when he saw the developing splendour of the Pier Pavilion, he set his hat at it as a venue more suited to his talents. He wore down the opposition and won the day. His orchestra trebled in size, as did his reputation. The old dog taught the new dog, in the shape of Sir Henry Wood, some tricks, and through the century there was a succession of famous names conducting, playing and performing at the Pavilion. Among them were Sir Adrian Boult, Sir Malcolm Sargent, Paul Beard and Sir Walford Davies. In later years it became almost exclusively a variety theatre with world-famous artistes. It was a venue for political conventions, and all the great orators and political leaders of the twentieth century trod its boards.

Pier Pavilion interior and orchestra, *c.* 1910.

The Grand Theatre, 2001. The author remembers this theatre as the place to go for excellent repertory productions in the 1950s and '60s: Agatha Christie, J.B. Priestley, Terence Rattigan and Noel Coward were the staple fare. Built in 1901, The Grand had an interesting time in the Second World War; it became part of the decentralised and dispersed BBC, and from its stage the nation's morale was bolstered by Tommy Handley, Sandy Powell and others. Eagerly awaited programmes, often disturbed by 'atmospherics', provided laughter in dark times. The theatre is now owned by the largest nightclub and disco company in Europe, Luminar Leisure. There are no more theatrical events but it is a valuable and well-run venue for the youth of North Wales. On three nights of the week up to 1,000 youngsters enjoy themselves in The Broadway Boulevard, which provides valuable employment for fifty people. We should be grateful that the century-old building is still standing, and is being preserved in the hands of responsible people.

Right: the Russian Ballet of St Petersburg. Each year on average, 200,000 tickets are sold for 340 performances at the new North Wales Theatre, which offers only the best in culture and entertainment. World-class artistes and companies vie for the opportunity to perform here, and the theatre draws crowds from all over North Wales, Cheshire and Merseyside. It holds an audience of 1,500 in an auditorium architecturally and technically honed to perfection. The programmes offered range from individual artistes to full-scale productions of travelling international shows. The annual visit of Welsh National Opera is an eagerly awaited event.

It is easy to run out of superlatives when describing the new North Wales Theatre. At the outset it must be said that its architecture is not to everyone's taste, but its opening in 1994 was a welcome reversal of a pattern of theatre and entertainment closures in the town, which had seemed unstoppable. The world-class facilities offered by this theatre cannot be rivalled in Wales, and are the envy of many larger towns in England. With its companion conference centre it adds a touch of class to what had hitherto been a drab stretch of the Promenade.

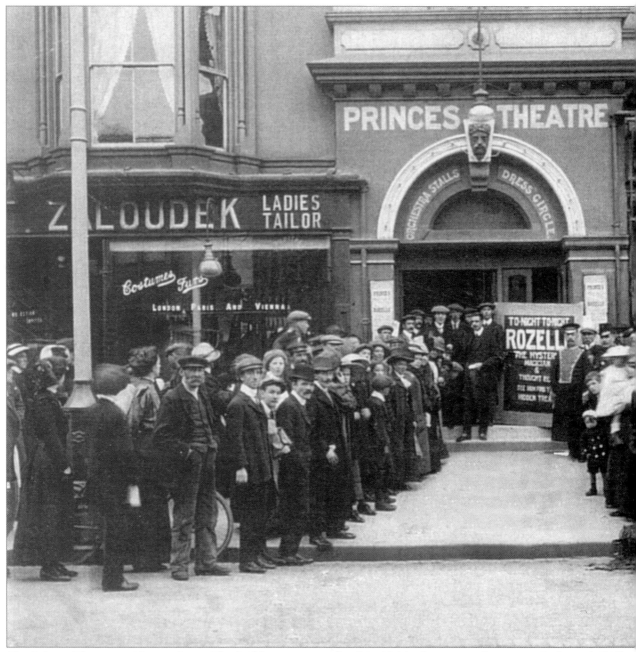

The Princes Theatre in Mostyn Street. The building was completed in 1864 when it was known as St George's Hall. As early as 1886 there was a protest meeting held here to kick against the Mostyn Estate's pernicious leasehold system, to little effect. In 1890 it was the venue for the Gilbert and Sullivan D'Oyly Carte Opera Company. In this photograph of the theatre the star is Rozello, 'The Mystery Magician and Thought Reader'. Its days as an entertainment venue, however, ended as a cinema. Llandudno had experience of the cinema early in its history; there was talk of an American style bioscope in the Pier Pavilion basement some time at the end of the nineteenth century. The early cinema played havoc with live theatre. Thousands of music halls either closed or were converted into cinemas because of the influence of the 'movies'. By 1929 only 100 music halls were competing for custom with 3,000 cinemas in Britain. It was estimated that about 75 per cent of professional musicians were employed in cinemas. They soon met their Nemesis in the shape of 'the talkies', which led to thousands being out of work almost overnight. The cinema was part of a revolution in the 1920s, when increasingly passive leisure activities such as the wireless and the gramophone were preparing a somnolent populace for the television era. The building is now a frozen food centre.

Poster showing the Savoy cinema, Mostyn Street. The Royal Oak Hotel once stood on this spot, and it was turned into a cinema at the outbreak of the First World War. This was early in terms of cinematic history since the first ever purpose-built cinema had opened in Colne, Lancashire only six years previously. It was during the First World War that cinemagoing became almost a national mania. By 1917 three and a half million people were going to the 'flea-pit' every day. There was a dramatic and destructive fire in the building in 1956 and it was extensively refurbished. The cinema closed in the 1980s, was purchased by Mr Billy Lal and is now a bargain centre and fast-food outlet.

The Savoy cinema in Mostyn Street, on the right of this photograph, *c.* 1938.

The Astra and Odeon Entertainment centre in 1934. Known as The Wintergardens, this complex was in Gloddaeth Street, a huge, architecturally monstrous building which provided a variety of venues for cinema, theatre, dances and conferences. It was built where once there had been a market garden specialising in fruit production, known locally as

The Vineyard. It cost its owners, coach operators, James and Zachary Brierley, £70,000 to build. The cinema section of the complex was taken over by the Odeon Company. It established a reputation as an opera house and was the venue for international opera and ballet companies. There were regular visits by the prestigious Welsh National Opera, founded in 1946. The complex was demolished in 1989 (left) and from then until the opening of the North Wales Theatre in 1994 Llandudno was virtually a cultural desert. The site is now occupied by a complex of retirement flats.

Gloddaeth Street with the Palladium and Wintergardens, 1946. The Palladium has been on the Gloddaeth Street site since 1920 when it replaced an early market hall built in 1864. Until recently the cinema had been struggling for years but lost the battle with diminishing audiences and was forced to close. It was bought by Wetherspoons, a company that specialises in purchasing old cinemas and turning them into 'theme pubs'. The abrupt closure of The Palladium gave rise to a great deal of concern and protest. The most vehement protestors had probably not been to the cinema for years. It must be acknowledged that the building, seen below, has, during the year 2001, been cleaned and refurbished in a way that reflects great credit to Wetherspoons. This company's aim is to preserve the ethos of the traditional British public house and to this end, it has banned jukeboxes, TVs, music and slot machines! It is a change for any company to purchase a property in the town and not follow up with widespread demolition or equally destructive apathy.

The Palladium today – a pub with a 'restoration' theme.

ACKNOWLEDGEMENTS

Special thanks to Tom and Eve Parry for their help, advice and good humoured encouragement during the writing of this book. Eirys Hughes was of considerable help with Welsh translations. Peter Roberts took many of the contemporary photographs. The Codman family were generous in the extreme with their time and unique original sources. Help was freely given by the following good friends: Derek Blamire, Stephen Brocket, Zoe Brocket, Roger Brown ARPS, Margot Catlin, John Cowell, Mike Day, Geoff Ellis, the late David Hughes, Bryan Hurst, Gareth Jones AM, Andrew Morley, Sue Morley, Glyn Morris, John Murgatroyd, Bill Oliver, Eifion W. Roberts, Llandudno Historical Society, the staff of Llandudno Library, and many others.

Opposite: To visit the cinema nowadays requires a trip out of town to Llandudno Junction where cinemagoers, starved for years, are enjoying an orgy of excellent films. The Cine UK Multiplex opened in 2001. Nine screens provide a choice of classic or contemporary films to a seating capacity of 1,630 patrons. Luxury dining out is available in one of the viewing areas with reclining seats and waitress service. There is a parking facility for hundreds of cars. The Chief Executive of this national company is an American, Steve Weiner, an enthusiast who has adopted an almost missionary zeal to the resurrection of the cinema throughout Great Britain. Some might complain about it as an example of creeping Americanism (it is surrounded by fast-food outlets), but it was badly needed in an area almost bereft of outside entertainment, and furthermore it provides work for sixty people in an area where jobs are few and far between.

FURTHER READING

Ivor Wynne Jones's *Llandudno, Queen of the Welsh Resorts* is the pivotal history of Llandudno and reading it in 1980 was an inspiration. Michael Senior's books have always been a source of pleasure and information. Other authors consulted were: F. Ron Williams, Aled Eames, F.C. Thornley, John Cowell, Don Smith, Keith Turner, Eifion W. Roberts, Mary Aris, Ian Skidmore, Diane and Nigel Bannerman, Llandudno Historical Society Publications. A recent book by Christopher Draper, *Walks from Llandudno*, is an informative and entertaining read in an original format, and is strongly recommended.

Mostyn Street, Llandudno, *c.* 1860.